PRAISE FOR *GENTLE ON MY MIND*

"I had the privilege of getting to know Glen, Kim, and their family while making the documentary, *Glen Campbell: I'll Be Me*. Like that film, *Gentle on My Mind* is written with grace, humor, and courageous candor. It's a beautiful love story, both heartbreaking and inspiring."

—JANE SEYMOUR

"In this candid and intimate memoir, my friend Kim Campbell reveals the ups and downs of her great love affair with Glen Campbell, a once-in-a-hundred-years talent. She writes in a wide-open, truthful, and sincere rhythm with great humor and pathos."

—JIMMY WEBB

"It seems that everybody writes a book at some point—and most should not be written. But when you're writing about an American legend, one of the most beloved musical icons in the history of our business, you have an obligation. Kim Campbell's *Gentle on My Mind* is a necessity. Sheryl and I (along with our kids, who grew up with Glen and Kim's) will always be attached to the Campbell Clan. That you could go to a backyard hillbilly Seder with Glen and me singing 'A Little Bit Country, A Little Bit Rock 'N Roll' as a finale, says something about our relationship. We were an unlikely pair. I will always miss golfing and laughing with Glen. This memoir will touch your heart and will give you an insight into Glen's career, his and Kim's family, and most of all their faith in Christ."

—ALICE COOPER

"Kim Campbell has given all of us who love Glen's musical legacy a real treasure. With what she has written here we get to know so much more of the man himself as well as the strength of their bond. And we get to know the woman who stood by him through the most profound and heartbreaking challenge of his life. Her willingness to let us into their life together—to share the moments of joy as well as despair—is an act of both love and courage. And it is alive with the spirit that anchors and sustains us all. It is a deeply human book."

—KEITH CARRADINE

"When I first met Kim, she had come to ask if we would make a film about Glen and his journey with Alzheimer's. What I discovered about this remarkable woman is her incredible patience and love for one of the great musicians of our time. I was fortunate to meet Glen at the beginning of his Alzheimer's journey. Together we shared his decline from this devastating disease. The film *Glen Campbell: I'll Be Me* shows what an incredible family Glen was blessed to have. I got to know the fantastic and brave Kim Campbell and her willingness to put Glen and her kids above all else. This book reflects her journey with Glen in a powerful and intimate way and gives great insight into what 'for better or for worse' means. Read it; you won't be disappointed."

—JAMES KEACH, FILMMAKER

"Kim writes with such candor, bravery, and deep description that you feel like you're in Glen Campbell's world with her. For his fans, the behind the scenes of that life is a fascinating gift. But rarely is anything more fascinating than a love story that has that conflicting dynamic of finding a soul mate and watching the one you love gradually disappear—in this case, becoming someone you don't always recognize, but still want to fiercely protect. This is Kim's story. A woman who chose faith, even when it seemed to break her heart. Absolutely enthralling."

—CHRISTI PAUL, CNN/HLN ANCHOR AND
AUTHOR OF *LOVE ISN'T SUPPOSED TO HURT*

"Kim Campbell has told a stunning story of love and sacrifice and how to live a life gracefully even in the face of unimaginable adversity."

—TREVOR ALBERT, FILMMAKER *GROUNDHOG
DAY* AND *GLEN CAMPBELL: I'LL BE ME*

GENTLE *on my* MIND

IN SICKNESS AND IN HEALTH
WITH GLEN CAMPBELL

KIM CAMPBELL

NELSON
BOOKS

An Imprint of Thomas Nelson

Published in Nashville, Tennessee, by Nelson Books, an imprint of Thomas Nelson. Nelson Books and Thomas Nelson are registered trademarks of HarperCollins Christian Publishing, Inc.

Thomas Nelson titles may be purchased in bulk for educational, business, fund-raising, or sales promotional use. For information, please e-mail SpecialMarkets@ ThomasNelson.com.

Unless otherwise noted, Scripture quotations are taken from the New King James Version®. © 1982 by Thomas Nelson. Used by permission. All rights reserved.

Scripture quotations marked CEB are from the Common English Bible. Copyright © 2011 Common English Bible.

Scripture quotations marked KJV are from the King James Version. Public domain.

Scripture quotations marked NIV are from the Holy Bible, New International Version®, NIV®. Copyright © 1973, 1978, 1984, 2011 by Biblica, Inc.® Used by permission of Zondervan. All rights reserved worldwide. www.Zondervan.com. The "NIV" and "New International Version" are trademarks registered in the United States Patent and Trademark Office by Biblica, Inc.®

Scripture quotations marked NLT are from the Holy Bible, New Living Translation. © 1996, 2004, 2007, 2013, 2015 by Tyndale House Foundation. Used by permission of Tyndale House Publishers, Inc., Carol Stream, Illinois 60188. All rights reserved.

Any Internet addresses, phone numbers, or company or product information printed in this book are offered as a resource and are not intended in any way to be or to imply an endorsement by Thomas Nelson, nor does Thomas Nelson vouch for the existence, content, or services of these sites, phone numbers, companies, or products beyond the life of this book.

ISBN 978-1-4002-1784-7 (eBook)
ISBN 978-1-4002-1783-0 (HC)

Library of Congress Control Number: 2020934936

Printed in the United States of America
20 21 22 23 24 LSC 10 9 8 7 6 5 4 3 2 1

CONTENTS

Introduction: My Life with Glen vii

Chapter 1   Unprepared 1
Chapter 2   Good Vibrations 19
Chapter 3   Despair 29
Chapter 4   White Firs and Ponderosa Pines 41
Chapter 5   By the Time We Got to Phoenix 61
Chapter 6   Denial and Determination 79
Chapter 7   The Shenandoah Valley 91
Chapter 8   Matthew 6:6 103
Chapter 9   Shorty and Mary 111
Chapter 10   The Tapes 119
Chapter 11   From Defeat to Defiance 127
Chapter 12   The Men's Grill 133
Chapter 13   Has Glen Campbell Converted to Judaism? 147
Chapter 14   Panic 155
Chapter 15   Water 167
Chapter 16   Campbellot 175
Chapter 17   Ghost on the Canvas 183

CONTENTS

Chapter 18   "I Need the Ones I Love, Lord"............................. 191

Chapter 19   A Dance of Love.. 201

Chapter 20   On the Line.. 207

Chapter 21   Power and Glory Forever............................... 219

Chapter 22   Deep Seclusion.. 231

Chapter 23   Music City... 239

Chapter 24   The Pell-Mell Bell..................................... 249

Chapter 25   Fractured Family...................................... 265

Chapter 26   Deeper Pain... 275

Chapter 27   A Better Place.. 281

Acknowledgments 288

About the Author.. 295

INTRODUCTION
My Life with Glen

G len and I loved dancing together. I loved how he held me in his arms. I loved how we moved as one.

"You're the dancer in the family," he told me. "I've spent my whole life on the bandstand, singing and playing my guitar, watching other folks dance. I never had the chance to dance."

"You're a good dancer," I assured him. "If you forget what comes next, just follow me." And he did. Glen danced through life with me for thirty-five years. Sometimes he led. Sometimes I led. It didn't matter. When God brought us together, we became "one flesh" (Mark 10:7–8 NIV).

Glen knew that dancing was not only my passion but my therapy. At the most challenging moments of my life, I turned to dance to express myself and work through my pain. I asked God to transform my grief into motion and cover me with joy. Each time, my prayer was answered. The poetry of Psalm 30 sprang to life: "You have turned my mourning into joyful danc-ing" (v. 11 NLT).

As a young woman, I began my professional life as a dancer, not realizing that there is something healing—even sacred—about bodily movement attuned to music and tempered with grace.

To be filled with grace is evidence of God's holy presence. At times of great suffering, it's easy to lose awareness of that pres-ence. Dancing always brought that awareness back.

For me, the dance metaphor goes deep. For this story, the dance metaphor is necessary. I say that because, although life with Glen entailed monumental struggles, those struggles were ultimately mitigated by movement. I came to learn that love, like dance, is all about movement. Love is never stagnant or motion-less. It bends, bows, and stretches. It expands and grows. Its essence is flexibility. Its beauty is divine. As a source of inspira-tion, dance strengthens me.

Enduring the enormous challenges placed before me required inspiration. That inspiration is rooted in love, but a love that can adapt to changing circumstances—a love, like dance, that is sup-ple, and yes, a love that is divine.

As you will soon see, this story is shaped by extreme emotions—fear and hope, pain and jubilation, despair and grati-tude. If I write from a gentle place, it is only because I serve a gentle God who has given me the grace to put pen to paper and share with you a journey that has brought me closer to him. And a goodbye that keeps Glen by rivers of my memory, ever smiling, ever gentle on my mind.

CHAPTER 1

UNPREPARED

It was my first and only blind date. I was blind to the excitement surrounding the man I was about to meet. He was blind to the young woman he had been told was attractive. I remember the date—May 28, 1981—because it looms large as the moment my life changed forever.

In a few weeks, I would turn twenty-three. I didn't know that Glen Campbell was forty-five. I didn't know much about him at all. I knew his name, of course, but at the height of his fame, when he starred in his own national TV show, I was ten years old and only vaguely aware of him. I didn't read the tabloids and knew nothing of his tumultuous romances and difficult divorces. I had no idea that he was fresh off a ten-month, knock-down, drag-out affair with fiery country star Tanya Tucker. Had I known, I might have bowed out before I bowed in. Sometimes ignorance is bliss. In this case, ignorance led to bliss.

The city was New York. The occasion was a James Taylor concert. James Taylor, along with the sublime Joni Mitchell, was an artist who always inspired me. The blind date had been set up through my friend Lynn Williford, whom I had met my freshman year at East Carolina University. Lynn was Miss Majorette of America and in many ways my role model. I'd been head majorette of my high school, but Lynn, with her dazzling twirls, spins, and spectacular behind-the-back catches, performed on another level. She was also stunningly beautiful—outrageously long eyelashes, big Bambi eyes, and a sweet disposition. I guess you could say Lynn and I both fit in that elusive All-American Girl category, although Lynn was in a category all her own.

At the 1981 Azalea Festival, she had been crowned Miss North Carolina, where she had the honor of introducing Glen Campbell and his band to the adoring throngs. That's where she met Carl Jackson, Glen's banjo player. They stayed in touch, and a few months later the Campbell crew was in New York. Lynn and I had also moved to the city where we were pursuing careers in dance. My world was ballet and Broadway, Mikhail Baryshnikov and Bob Fosse. Yes, I admit it, I loved Liza Minnelli. I also had a crazy schedule: ballet classes in the morning and dancing two shows a day with the Rockettes at Radio City Music Hall. I even managed to squeeze in a jazz class in between shows. I was dancing seven hours a day. I weighed 101 pounds and ate a pint of Häagen-Dazs every day. Ah, the joys of being young!

Through Carl Jackson, Lynn made the arrangements for our date. For the first and only time, I told my dance captain I was sick and couldn't make the evening performance. To be brutally honest, my main motivation was to see James Taylor. I was far more a fan of folk and Southern rock than mainstream country music. At the same time, I knew that Glen was a star. The prospect of meeting a star is always alluring. I was curious.

The date was unconventional, but then again, everything about my life with Glen became unconventional. Why should our first encounter be any different? Carl and Lynn took me to the Waldorf Astoria where Glen was staying with his parents. Carl said earlier that day Glen had taken his folks to see Mickey Rooney and Ann Miller in *Sugar Babies*. I was impressed. Glen was apparently a good son.

We went up to his suite where we waited in the lavish living room. Only a few minutes passed before he burst into the room singing "Rhinestone Cowboy"! *Quite an entrance. Quite a man,* I thought. He was tall, blond, and handsome. His sandy hair was perfectly in place. His soft beard was neatly trimmed. His light-blue silk shirt mirrored his light-blue eyes. His zippered boots were crafted of black ostrich. His voice projected an intoxicating mixture of mellifluousness and enthusiasm. When his eyes met mine, I felt myself melting—just a bit. And then a bit more when he said, "Carl, why didn't you tell me she was so pretty!"

Music to my ears. It didn't sound like a line, though. Glen sounded sincere. His sincerity, in fact, was so strong—along with his sexiness—that, while I was normally a composed young woman, I felt nervous, shy, and even intimidated.

The presence of his parents took off the edge. Like me, they came from a small country town. Down-to-earth, good-hearted folks without a bit of pretension. They made me feel safe.

Dinner at Peacock Alley, in the marble-columned, palm-tree-décor lobby of the Waldorf, was somewhat overwhelming. Until that night, the New York I knew was a city of coffee shops and delis where struggling actors and dancers like me dined on tuna fish and meat loaf. Peacock Alley was the epitome of elegant refinement. I did not feel elegant, I did not feel refined, but I did feel a magnetism coursing between me and Glen. Was I inventing that dynamic? Was I fantasizing that this man seemed to be as drawn to me as I was to him? Maybe. But maybe not. During dinner he couldn't have been more solicitous. He peppered me with questions about my past. His queries weren't pushy; they were genuinely sweet; he seemed genuinely interested. I wished I had known more about his career, but he was happy to keep the attention on me.

When the food arrived, Glen bowed his head and said a simple blessing. That humble gesture caught me by surprise.

With hesitation I asked Glen, "Are you a Christian?"

"Yes," he said with a note of honest conviction in his voice.

At that moment, I flashed back to something that had happened a week earlier. I had been walking down Fifth Avenue with two girlfriends I had danced with in Disney's Broadway show *Snow White* before landing my current job at Radio City. With a fairy tale involving a handsome prince in recent memory, we were wistfully wishing for a man of our dreams.

One of them offered up a prayer, "Dear God, please send me my Prince Charming." The other friend looked up and said, "Dear God, please send me my knight in shining armor!" When it was my turn I thought about it for a minute and then half-jokingly prayed out loud, "Dear God, please send me a handsome, Southern, Christian, uh let me think . . . millionaire . . . to fall in love with!" Now here I was, having dinner with a handsome, Southern, Christian millionaire. Was meeting Glen a serious answer to my half-serious prayer?

It was starting to look like it, especially when we arrived at the theater where flash bulbs were popping, paparazzi were screaming Glen's name, and fans were reaching out for autographs. Glen put his arm around me protectively and ushered me to our seats. James Taylor was great. He sang "Fire and Rain," "Sweet Baby James," and all his beautiful songs.

I must admit it was hard to focus on James Taylor while sitting next to Glen. Glen was six feet one, and in his younger days, he had trained to be Mr. Albuquerque; he still had that muscular physique. His deep and resonant voice commanded my attention. I was smitten with his smile, his voice, and his smell.

Afterward, Glen escorted me backstage. James greeted Glen like a long-lost friend. Glen introduced me like a newfound friend. As we walked to the exit, Glen stopped, gently pressed me against the wall, and kissed me. The kiss was long, passionate, and heavenly. I was breathless. I felt like I was dreaming. I was seated in the back of a limo when Glen kissed me again. I didn't resist. I couldn't resist. The lights of Midtown Manhattan illuminated Glen's face.

"This the best first date ever," he said.

"For me too," I had to admit.

I'd been on many dates with surfers and frat boys. But I had never felt like I'd been with a grown man. Glen was a grown man—and then some. Back at his suite, though, the sweetness of this dream date began to sour. Glen began to drink. And drink. And drink some more. The evening, begun on a light cloud of charm, was suddenly darkening. I fought the darkness. I didn't want to see what I was seeing. This man turned me on. I wanted the turn-on to last. I allowed a few more kisses, and yes, I was aroused. But no, I couldn't deny that he was sloppy drunk.

Then he whispered in my ear, "I want to jump your bones." I pulled back.

"What?" I asked incredulously, hoping he did not say what I thought he said.

"I want to jump your bones," he repeated softly.

I had never been spoken to that way before. I felt vulnerable and a little frightened, alone in the room with an intoxicated, much-older man. I could see I was in a bad situation and had no business remaining there.

"It's getting late," I said

"If you go home now, you'll never see me again," he warned.

I was shocked. Right in front of my eyes, my Prince Charming had turned into a big fat toad. As for the Christian millionaire I had prayed for—without Christian values, all the treasures in his kingdom couldn't persuade me to stay. I decided to ignore his remark and make my way to the door as gracefully as possible.

"I enjoyed meeting you and your parents," I said with a smile. "Thank you for the concert."

As the door shut behind me, I didn't know what to think. He had begun the evening as one person and turned into another. Little did I know that transformation would become the central and most critical challenge of our relationship.

That first night I was convinced there would be no relationship. And yet, minutes after arriving back at my apartment, the phone was ringing off the hook.

"I'm sorry," said Glen, his voice now soft and strangely sober. Maybe he had been drinking coffee. Maybe he had come to his senses. "I want to see you again. I want you to know how bad I feel for the way I behaved."

What could I say? What *did* I say?

I said, "Well, I appreciate the apology."

"And I'd appreciate a second chance. Let me at least take you to dinner tomorrow night. I'll be on my best behavior."

"You better," I said, half-jokingly, half-seriously.

My head was filled with misgivings. My body was filled with longing. My spirit was filled with confusion. This man was, all at once, wonderful and bewildering. He had displayed exquisite manners and then turned vulgar. I wanted to dwell on the exquisite manners. I wanted to forget the vulgarity and simply blame it on the drinking. I wanted to accept his invitation, and I did.

When I arrived at Radio City the next day to do the matinee, the dance captain was waiting for me. From the tone of his voice, I knew I'd been busted.

"Feeling better?" he asked as he handed me the *New York Post* with a splashy photo of me and Glen leaving the James Taylor concert. The paper called me Glen's "mystery beauty." I'd be lying to say I didn't like reading those words. Fortunately, my dance captain was a Glen Campbell fan.

"Don't' worry," he said. "All is forgiven. Anyone would be crazy to turn down a date with that man."

Relieved, I went upstairs to get ready for the show. I was just putting on my false eyelashes when the dressing room phone rang. One of the other dancers answered the phone. With a bewildered look on her face, she said, "Kim, it's for you—it's *People* magazine! They want to know about your date with Glen Campbell." None of them knew I had gone out with Glen the night before. As I took the phone, they all pressed in; they wanted to know the details.

"Yes, this is Kim. I'm a dancer here. My last name is spelled *W-o-o-l-l-e-n*. I'm twenty-two. Okay. Thanks!" I hung up the phone. That was it, short and sweet.

"You went out with Glen Campbell?" the girls pried. "Are you going out with him again?"

"Well, we're supposed to have dinner tonight," I said, trying to make little of it. I was afraid to make more of it in case it didn't work out. But I realized then that dating Glen was a big deal.

After the show I hurriedly stripped off my sequins and put on a striped silk dress. The phone rang again, and the same girl answered. "It's the doorman, Kim. He says Glen Campbell is here to pick you up." All the girls rushed to the windows to take a peek. I quickly put on my heels, grabbed my purse, and rushed to the elevators to make my way down to the street. The driver opened the car door, and I slid in to sit next to Glen. He looked amazing!

"Hi there," he said with a charismatic smile before kissing my hand. "Thank you for giving me a second chance. I hope you like the 21 Club."

"What's the 21 Club?" I asked, wondering if he was just making fun of how young I was.

"It's a famous restaurant at 21 West Fifty-Second Street," he said with a smile. The driver added that back in the prohibition era, it was a popular New York speakeasy that had since become a legendary restaurant where ambassadors dined with opera divas.

I had never been to such a prestigious and glamorous restaurant. The centerpiece of our corner table was an assortment of white roses floating in a sculpted vase. The fragrance was dizzying. The food was divine. The lights were soft. So was Glen's voice. He drank a glass of white wine and nothing more.

Glen's curiosity about me was undaunted. But after the tuna tartare, tortellini lamb ragout, coq au vin, English pea puree, almond strawberry cheesecake, and café latte, I felt confident enough to ask questions of my own. In these pre-Google days, there was no way to research the man sitting next to me. I knew virtually nothing of his past. As naive as my questions sounded—as naive as I was—there were things I wanted to know.

"Have you ever been married before?" I asked.

"Unfortunately, yes," he said. "Three times."

This seemed unfathomable to me, as though he had already lived three lifetimes before meeting me. I swallowed before continuing.

"Do you have children?"

"Five," he replied.

That should have sent me running for the door.

"How old are they?" I gulped.

I was shocked to learn that Glen had one child who was actually older than me and that another was only a baby. If one of his children was older than me, how old was he? With much trepidation I asked, "How old are you?"

"Forty-five." He smiled.

Forty-five sounded ancient to me. He was a full year older than my dad. I suddenly felt uncomfortable being wooed by someone that age, even if he was gorgeous, talented, and famous. The rational part of my brain was sounding alarm sirens. At the same time, my heart was making excuses and rationalizations to justify pursuing the relationship because, despite all common sense and my many misgivings, I was falling head over heels.

I didn't know what to think. When you're a twenty-two-year-old dancer, in love with the arts, and on a date with a famous artist lavishing attention on you, I'm not sure you're thinking straight. Actually, I'm not sure I was thinking at all. That came later. I was feeling.

Feeling privileged.

Feeling glamorous.

Feeling light-headed.

And, of course, feeling confused.

In the limo back to the apartment, we held hands and didn't speak. Glen was a sensitive soul, and he knew I'd need time to absorb everything I'd just learned about him. He also knew that the previous night's drunken behavior required ongoing repair. In front of my apartment building, he leaned over to kiss me. The kiss was passionate. We were both aroused, but he backed off and simply said, "Would it be okay if I called you tomorrow?"

I heard his request as undoubtedly sincere. I didn't hesitate. I said, "Yes, it would be okay."

That night I tossed and turned. Never in my wildest dreams had I ever expected to date a man with five children. It was crazy. Made no sense. Was definitely a situation to avoid. And yet.

At times *yet* can be the most powerful word in the world. Yet I felt something in him so good, so genuine, so affectionate, so intimate, so irresistible that I found myself rationalizing.

Was it really such a big deal to be dating a man older than my father? It obviously wasn't normal—I did not need anyone to tell me that—but maybe there were times when exceptions were understandable. I needed outside advice. Deciding I'd better talk this over with my father, I called him the next day. I felt very awkward as I began. "Daddy, uh . . . I'm dating this man who is twenty-two years older than me. He has been married three times and has five children. One of them is older than me, and one is a baby. Do you think that's okay?"

"Who is this man?" my dad demanded. His voice sounded stern and skeptical.

"It's Glen Campbell," I said.

"Glen Campbell? The entertainer?" he asked in disbelief.

"Yes," I replied in all seriousness.

He went silent for a moment and then responded with matter-of-fact optimism, "It's fine, just fine! Age is just a number!"

I was a little surprised by his response. Our conversation kind of reminded me of the dad from the movie *Arthur* who, upon hearing that his daughter, played by Liza Minnelli, was dating a notorious alcoholic millionaire, played by Dudley Moore, brushed aside all objections. I know it sounds like my dad was setting aside sound judgment, but he didn't know Glen had a drinking problem, and I think he was just relieved I wasn't dating another surfer or struggling actor. I think he viewed it as a truly unique situation; and, after all, anyone in his age group was a huge Glen Campbell fan by default! So there it was. I had my dad's blessing.

My father's blessing meant a great deal. I was looking for approval. I needed someone I respected to assure me that I was not being foolish.

The truth is, I was falling in love for the first time in my life. The truth is, I wanted this man, body and soul. The truth is, as a twenty-two-year-old woman, I was overwhelmed by my feelings for this man.

Today, as I remember what was going through my mind during those early days of my romance with Glen, I can truthfully say that it wasn't my mind driving me. It was my heart. Glen had won my heart. And though my heart was broken time and again, I have no regrets—not a single one—about my ultimate decision to follow my heart. I say that because I know, for all the complications to follow, I was driven by love.

Glen was unrelenting. He did everything he could to sweep me off my feet. That first week in New York was a whirlwind of limousines, flowers, fine dining, and shows. The paparazzi went wild every time we showed up in public. One night as we cozied up in our booth to watch Tom Jones perform at the Savoy, an aggressive photographer began flashing away at our table. The lights were blinding. I was intimidated. Glen gave him a gesture to make it clear that he did not appreciate the intrusion. That same week we attended Brooke Shields's sixteenth birthday party. I'd seen her big hit, *The Blue Lagoon*, the year before, and now, sitting next to her at the dais, she was telling me that her next film, *Endless Love*, would be out later in the summer. She was a gorgeous young woman who handled her fame with remarkable composure. She spoke to me as if I were a friend.

Celebrities were everywhere, but I was focused on Glen. He was focused on me. He was attentive, he was caring, he was attuned to my nervousness in this new world and did all he could to put me at ease. He also asked if he could see me perform at Radio City. Anxiously, I agreed.

One of the numbers featured me as a baton twirler in front of the Rockettes. Twirling was my specialty, but I was nonetheless afraid my fingers would become sweaty. I could see myself dropping the baton for the first time. Fortunately, I didn't. I nailed the routine. I was really just a chorus girl, but the fact that Glen wanted to see me perform meant the world to me. Afterward, Glen was effusive.

"You were wonderful," he said. "You are wonderful. You will be wonderful." I enjoyed the steamy innuendo but more importantly his willingness to wait.

With sex put on the back burner, I felt more comfortable around him. He made no moves. He called every day. Dinner every night. Passionate kissing in the back of the limo—what could be more romantic? But that was it. He wanted more, and of course I did, too, but I was grateful for his restraint. When it came to generosity, though, Glen was not restrained. He wanted to take me shopping, buy me jewelry, even offered to buy me a car. What would I do with a car in Manhattan? I politely refused. I said I didn't want to feel bought. He explained that wasn't his intention. I believed him. I merely said that I really wasn't comfortable with extravagant gifts. He understood. He never mentioned gifts again.

But he did mention a show in Philadelphia. He was performing there.

Had I ever seen his show?

No.

Had I ever heard him sing?

On records, of course, but I honestly said I wasn't all that familiar with his music. That made him feel better. He knew I was falling for him, not his status as a star.

But, in any case, would I come to Philadelphia to see his show? Would I spend the weekend there? Would I stay with him at the city's most glamorous hotel?

"You're asking whether I'll sleep with you?"

"I guess that's just what I'm asking," he admitted.

"I don't think so," I said. "It's still too early, but I do want to see your show. And I'd love to stay with you in Philadelphia."

Was I giving him a double message? No to sex but yes to staying in his room? Despite my ambivalence—or maybe because of it—he said, "Whatever you like, darling. I just wanna be with you."

Glen arrived in Philly early for rehearsals. He sent a stretch limo for me. During the drive down the Garden State Parkway, I had time to think things over. I had packed some sexy lingerie. I did so because, well, I wanted to look alluring. I wanted Glen to want me. I'm afraid that in writing all this, I sound manipulative. Maybe I was. But the deeper truth is, I already knew Glen wanted me. I guess I just wanted him to want me even more. And yet I was also determined to keep my pledge to not have sex.

By the time I arrived in Philly, I was feeling scared and insecure. So much had happened so quickly. When Glen saw me backstage, he rushed over, picked me up, swung me around, and gave me a big kiss. He introduced me to his band. Everyone was welcoming and extra kind. I think that's because they were relieved that he was no longer seeing Tanya Tucker. In these past days, I'd heard and read more about their fling. Reports said it was fueled by cocaine and booze. His closest friends called her the devil. In comparison, I, a former majorette and a newly hired Radio City dancer, seemed like an innocent angel. In fact, *angel* was the word Glen insisted on calling me.

I sat third row center for the show. I was floored. Perhaps because I got to know the man before I knew the music, the music seemed a perfect extension of his soul. The music soared. I'd thought I might simply have to tolerate it, but I loved it. Without reservation. Loved "Wichita Lineman." Loved "By the Time I Get to Phoenix." Loved "Southern Nights." Loved "Galveston." Loved "Rhinestone Cowboy." He sang with such conviction. In his music, his pleasing personality had added force. He connected with his audience because he related to them with natural charm. He was one of them. He wasn't haughty. He didn't strut or swagger. He simply sang his heart out, and his fans loved him for it. I loved him for it. That evening, hearing him perform for the first time, I loved him more than ever.

That night in his hotel I wanted to reward him with the gift of myself. But I had made that pledge. The pledge stuck in my mind, even as we shared a bottle Glen's favorite wine, Louis Jadot Pouilly-Fuissé, even as I went into the bathroom and changed into my new negligee.

"Stop," said Glen when he saw me. "Stand still."

"Why?"

"I need to keep this picture in my mind. I said you're an angel. Now you really do look like an angel. Turn around."

I did a slow complimentary soutenu turn. Before I could complete the turn, he smiled mischievously and said, "I can see through your gown."

I was glad.

I slipped into bed. We cuddled and kissed. The sensation of his skin. The strength of his arms. The beauty of his eyes peering in mine. The arousal was more than we could bear and yet we bore it. We restrained from the ultimate act. Glen understood that my pledge was serious. I wanted him to respect me. I wanted him to know I had boundaries. And he wanted me to know that he could accept those boundaries. It was frustrating but also beautiful. We fell asleep in each other's arms.

In the morning, I awoke after Glen. He voiced no anger that our love had not been consummated. He expressed no incriminations, no guilt-squeezing, no regrets. We had breakfast in bed. The next thing I knew we were back in a limo driving to Tuxedo Park, forty miles north of Manhattan, where songwriter Jimmy Webb lived in a mansion behind a gated community that once housed banker J. P. Morgan and author Mark Twain. The fairy tale in which I found myself grew more fabulous by the minute.

CHAPTER 2

GOOD VIBRATIONS

In high school, I had played first-chair piccolo on the song "MacArthur Park" and first-chair flute on "Didn't We" without knowing that Jimmy Webb had composed both songs. I didn't know so much. I didn't know that mansions actually had names. Webb's was called Renamor. I had never seen a house so big, much less been inside one. I couldn't help but gawk at the old-world grandiosity and glamour of it all. Not that Jimmy put on airs. Just the opposite. He greeted us wearing jeans and a tattered T-shirt. He was as down-to-earth as Glen. Beforehand, Glen had told me Jimmy had written "Wichita Lineman," "By the Time I Get to Phoenix," "Galveston," and "Honey Come Back"—all smash hits. The list went on and on: "Up, Up and Away" by the 5th Dimension, "Adios" by Linda Ronstadt, "All I Know" by Art Garfunkel.

We went to the living room where a nine-foot Steinway grand was the focal point. Guitar in hand, Glen sat next to him at the piano bench. I sat on a couch only a few feet away. Shafts of sunlight poured in through the windows, casting both men in an aura of radiance. The moment was almost cimenatic as Jimmy swept his hands over the piano and Glen ran his fingers across the frets of his guitar. The soundtrack they provided was more than romantic; it was spiritual. They were obviously soul brothers, brothers in sound and artistic expression whose essence was rooted in love. I might have been a naive young woman wildly in love, but if you had been in that lovely living room on that lovely summer afternoon—no matter your age or life experience—I'm certain that you would have felt the same.

They spoke with their instruments, and they spoke freely. Jimmy had an idea for a new song. He had a melody and the beginning of a story. Hearing the notes and the lyrics, Glen sang it as though he had been singing that song his entire life. Their rapport was magical.

At one point, Jimmy stopped playing, turned to me, and said, "This man has been telling me you're the best thing that's ever happened to him—and I believe him—but how much do you really know about him?"

"Whoa, Jimmy," said Glen. "Don't tell her too much. Right now she thinks I'm a good guy."

"Not just a good guy, Kim, but a certified genius. Everyone knows he's about the best singer out there. Everyone knows he's a great entertainer who puts on a great show. Everyone knows his hits—"

"Most of them written by you, Jimmy."

"But did you know, Kim, that you're looking at probably the best all-around guitarist on the planet? No exaggeration. Reminds me of Nat Cole. Nat Cole was one of the premier pianists of his time, but he was also a brilliant singer. Once his hits came fast and furiously, fans forgot about his piano playing. Same with Glen. Has he ever told you about his days as a session player in LA?"

"No," I said.

"Kim doesn't wanna hear all that stuff," said Glen.

"Sure I do."

"He wasn't just a guitar session player," Jimmy continued.

"He was *the* guitar session player. Tell her the records you played on, Glen."

"Come on, Jimmy. Kim doesn't need a history lesson."

"Yes I do," I said.

"Did you know Brian Wilson of the Beach Boys wrote a song called 'Guess I'm Dumb' just for Glen?" Jimmy asked.

"Somehow that doesn't seem so flattering at the moment," Glen said with a laugh.

"Glen played on the Beach Boys album *Pet Sounds*, actually *became* a Beach Boy, and toured with the group. Talk about good vibrations—girls were chasing him down like he was Elvis."

Glen grinned his ah-shucks grin, but Jimmy kept talking.

"Sinatra used him on 'Strangers in the Night.' Phil Spector, maybe the most radical producer in pop music, used him when he cut the Righteous Brothers singing 'You've Lost That Loving Feeling.' Then there's Ricky Nelson, the Monkees, Dean Martin, the Mamas and Papas, Jan and Dean . . ."

"He recorded with all those artists?"

"That's only a few. But it isn't just the astounding number of artists and sessions he played on, it's the variety of styles he's mastered."

"Hey, man," said Glen to Jimmy. "You're boring this poor lady to death."

"This lady," he said, "is learning things she needs to know."

"I'm not sure," said Glen.

"I am," I said. "I'm interested in everything about you."

"There you go," said Jimmy. "I'm not sure you deserve anyone this sharp, Glen, but now that your country-boy charm has won her over, she deserves to get the lowdown on you."

"As long as you're talking about the musical lowdown," said

Glen. "She probably already knows too much about the other stuff."

"The other stuff doesn't matter," said Jimmy. "The music is all there is. Man, you *are* music. You tell Kim about Elvis?"

"You knew Elvis?" I asked Glen.

"Me and Elvis were brought up the same way—picking cotton and looking at the north end of a southbound mule."

"Tell Kim about *Viva Las Vegas*," Jimmy urged.

"No big deal. Elvis was about to record the soundtrack and needed a picker. I was the picker he chose. Turned out Elvis remembered me from years earlier when I was playing in a band led by my uncle Dick. He and I came back to Elvis's dressing room in Albuquerque when Elvis opened for Faron Young. The girls were so crazy they broke down the door just for a chance to touch Elvis. The cops had to come. But Elvis being Elvis, he kept his cool. He had me play some guitar licks for him and he was real supportive. 'Your nephew can really play that thing,' he told Uncle Dick."

"Now here's the thing," said Jimmy. "Your man here, for all his astounding virtuosity, cannot read or write a note of music."

"Then how does he do it?" I asked.

"Ear. All ear. Plays country by ear. Rock by ear. Jazz by ear. Pop by ear. Did he tell you who his master is?"

"No."

"Django Reinhardt, the gypsy guitarist who revolutionized the guitar. Django was this crazy genius who lost two of his fingers in a fire. He found a way to overcompensate by inventing voicings, rhythms, and melodic lines that took Paris by storm—and later, America. Louis Armstrong loved him. Duke Ellington loved him. Willie Nelson loved him. And Glen became his greatest disciple."

"Is he still alive?"

"Oh, no, baby," said Glen, starting to play a Django song on his guitar. "He died in 1953. I was sixteen or seventeen, playing in Albuquerque with my uncle's band, Dick Bills and the Sandia Mountain Boys. I only knew him from his records. But man, I memorized them. I knew those suckers cold."

Glen broke into a song that had me mesmerized. I'd never heard anything like it before, this haunting melody played over a Spanish-sounding groove that suggested a mystery that was both light and dark. Glen sang, not with his voice, but his guitar. His guitar cried and laughed at the same time. He played the song with such simplicity and tenderhearted warmth that I was speechless.

After he was through, Jimmy and I sat in silence.

"Was I exaggerating?" Jimmy asked me.

"No, you weren't. That was stunning. What's it called?"

"'Nuages,'" said Glen, pointing out the window. "It means clouds."

I glanced though the window at the trail of low-hanging white clouds passing over the sun. At that moment I was over-whelmed with a feeling of love I had never felt before. It took all the restraint I possessed not to burst out and scream, "Glen Campbell, I love you!"

Luckily, just before I overheated, the doorbell rang. It was Jud Strunk, a close friend to Glen and Jimmy Webb and another good ol' boy, country-bred and sweet as pie. He started out as a banjo player, reinvented himself as a singer-songwriter, and had a big hit, "Daisy a Day." Best of all, Jud was a comic, corny but hilari-ous. He'd played a country bumpkin on *Laugh-In*. Beyond the humor, though, these three buddies broke into a deep discussion about the mysteries of music. These were highly intelligent men who understood the intricacies and nuances of composition, whether it entailed a melody, lyric, or even a joke. The stories never stopped, especially those about their sessions, with everyone from Richard Harris to Harry Nilsson. They spoke about singer-songwriter Roger Miller as the wittiest man to ever walk the earth. Jud also talked about his vintage plane, a Fairchild M-62A, that he'd just restored.

"Got a parachute for that flying tin can?" asked Glen.

"No need," answered Jud.

"Hey, flyboy," said Jimmy, "there'll be a big need if something goes wrong."

"Everything's going right," said Jud.

"Maybe so, buddy," said Glen, "but I'm getting you the best parachute money can buy."

"Hold up," said Jimmy, who left the table only to return a few minutes later with a parachute he just happened to have.

Uproarious laughter all around.

"Take it with you," said Glen. "The world can afford to lose the plane, but the world can't afford to lose you."

"You're a good man, Glen Campbell," said Jud.

"You know how I met this man of yours?" Jimmy asked me.

I was so pleased to hear the expression "this man of yours" that I was almost too flushed to answer. Yet I managed to say, "No. Please tell me."

"Well, long story short, I'm the son of an Okie Baptist preacher. Learned music by arranging hymns in church. Far as music went, all I knew were those blessed hymns. Then one day I was driving the tractor—couldn't have been older than fourteen—with this tinny transistor radio dangling down from the umbrella over my head. Then here comes this song—'Turn Around, Look at Me.' I 'bout fell off the tractor. The song pierced my heart and so did the voice of the singer, Glen Campbell. That night I went to bed and, sure as the three of you are sitting here next to me, I got on my knees and asked God to one day let me write a song half as good as that one and, if God could work it out, let the song be sung by Glen Campbell."

"Well, sir," said Jud, "Looks like God worked it out."

Jimmy laughed. "He sure did. Over the next few years, I'd write at least a hundred songs half as good as 'Turn Around, Look at Me.' And within four years, I'd have a hit on the charts with Glen Campbell."

"While God was blessing you, Jimmy," said Glen, "he was blessing me even more."

Talk of music. Talk of God. Feelings of beautiful fellowship among men with artistic souls. And there I was, privileged to witness it all, feeling so blessed myself to have learned so much more about this man who continued to fascinate and excite me on every possible level.

On the ride back to Manhattan, Glen was especially mellow.

"Ain't those guys great?" he asked me.

"Wonderful," I said.

"Jimmy kept going on about me, but that dude is a true-enough genius. Without him, I'd never have this career. You'll be seeing a lot more guys like Jimmy and Jud. You'll be seeing everyone, Kim. You'll be seeing the kind of world God has opened up for me."

I squeezed Glen's hand and leaned over to kiss him on the cheek. His beard felt fuzzy and soft against my lips. For the rest of the ride we stayed silent. The highway was humming. The night birds were singing. A crescent moon, a sky crowded with stars, a man and woman at the beginning of a life I knew would be filled with love.

"I'm falling in love with you, baby," said Glen when we arrived at my apartment building. "I hope you know that."

"I don't know it," I said. "But I feel it."

We kissed, and kissed again, and then again. Though sex was on our minds, sex wasn't mentioned. Glen knew what I was thinking. He knew I wanted to wait—if only just a bit longer. He was considerate enough not push the point.

He walked me upstairs and stood at the door. We kissed a final time.

"I'll call you first thing tomorrow."

"Promise?"

"With all my heart."

That evening I slept like a baby. My old reservations fell away into serene dreams of fields covered with daisies.

I awoke early. I made myself coffee and was hoping that before I went off to ballet class, Glen would call, just to say good morning. But he didn't. He didn't call that morning. He didn't call that evening. He didn't call the next day or day after.

He disappeared.

Without so much as a goodbye.

Not a single call or a single word.

He was gone.

Utterly gone.

CHAPTER 3

DESPAIR

I have learned in life that it is God and God alone who saves us from despair. At twenty-two, I had not learned that lesson. At twenty-two, I had been convinced that I had met my Prince Charming, my knight in shining armor, and my Southern Christian millionaire all wrapped in one incredible man. At twenty-two, I was certain I was about to live happily ever after. I was adrift and yet hopelessly in love.

Hopeless is an interesting word. Today I feel that the mere presence of God negates the idea of hopelessness. But back then, all I knew was that this man, who had made me believe that he loved me, had left me. Not merely left me, but done so callously.

"Honey," said one of my fellow dancers at Radio City, "I'm afraid he's just dropped you."

"I'm afraid you're right," I had to agree.

I wondered: Was it the fact that I had denied him sex? If that was the case, then fine. Let him go. Because if sex was all he had wanted, then I had been saved from a relationship that would have inevitably failed. Yet when I thought back to our dates, to our long talks, and especially to the beautiful day we spent with Jimmy and Jud, I knew in my heart of hearts that Glen saw me as more than an object of physical desire. I was absolutely sure that our union was soul-to-soul. In fact, he even said. "You're my soul mate, Kim. A soul mate I thought would never come my way."

And yet facts are facts. The phone didn't ring. The postman didn't deliver a letter. Days dragged by. I accepted—or at least tried to accept—the fact that I had been hoodwinked. Duped. Dumped.

And then Daddy called.

"I guess you already know what I'm about to tell you."

"Know what?"

"About Glen."

My heart raced. "Is he all right?"

"He's back with Tanya Tucker."

"How do you know that?"

"He and Tanya are on the cover of every tabloid in the supermarket."

My heart went from racing to sinking.

"You want me to read what it says?" asked my father.

"No."

"Well, you're right not to aggravate yourself. I know you're heartbroken, sweetheart, but I do believe my little girl dodged a bullet. Sounds like there's two Glen Campbells. You met the good guy. But the bad guy is out there on the loose. And it sounds like the bad guy is really bad."

I put down the phone and cried.

Glen later put it succinctly when he said, "I got more press during the fifteen months I dated Tanya than during my previous thirteen-year career where I'd sold over thirty million records."

The thing that stung most was that Glen had told me after twelve months of being with Tanya, he was through. Like me, Tanya was twenty-two. Unlike me, Tanya was a star. Also unlike me, Tanya was a brawler—and proud of it. She boasted about drinking and drugging. Glen called that affair toxic. Yet, in spite of the toxicity—or maybe because of it—for a full year they couldn't stay away from each other. The tabloids talked about verbal and physical abuse, Tanya's as well as Glen's. They tore up hotel rooms. They crashed out on cocaine. Glen called Tanya an addiction worse than cocaine. God only knows what Tanya said about Glen.

After meeting Glen, I learned the broad outline of this story but not the gory details. All his friends kept telling me was, "You're saving this guy. He's finally found a woman who can pull him out of the pigpen."

Those comments meant little to me because I couldn't imagine him in a pigpen. Our first night aside, I had put him on a pedestal. He had displayed nothing but kindness and consideration. I was certain the chapter that preceded me had closed. He had turned the page. We were turning the page together. We were writing a new book—a book of true love. And now this.

What to believe? None of it. All of it.

"Maybe it's not as bad as all that," said one of my friends. "Or maybe it's worse. But usually when there's smoke there's fire."

I cried myself to sleep every night for weeks. After all, hearts are delicate. I was entitled. I prayed that Glen would call and apologize. I prayed that God would do this or do that to bring him back to me. But God didn't seem to be listening. I was super depressed.

All I could do was put the whole thing out of my mind. Move on. Chalk it up to the biggest miscalculation I had ever made. I thought back over my life. I made a list of things for which I was grateful. I was grateful to be Kimberly Woollen, born June 18, 1958. Grateful to be a believer. Grateful that my dad married my mom, who grew up in Mill Creek, North Carolina. They met when Dad was stationed in the military in North Carolina and, after their wedding, decided to plant roots in Indiana, my father's home state. Mom worked as a newspaper editor in Indianapolis to help pay for Dad's education. Ultimately, he earned a master's in health administration. She was a loyal wife whose loyalty was not rewarded. My early life was ruptured by my parents' divorce. It happened suddenly and unexpectedly when I was ten and my sister Pamela was three.

Knowing that I was a conscientious Girl Scout, Daddy took me to the Girl Scout store and told me to pick out whatever I wanted. This was an unusual treat. I picked out a Girl Scout watch that Dad was happy to buy. On the drive home, I kept admiring my new watch on my wrist, but felt something wasn't quite right. I didn't know exactly what was happening but found out when we pulled into the driveway.

He basically gave his version of the Sonny and Cher song, "Better Sit Down Kids," in which a father tells his kids that he's divorcing Mom. The difference was that in the song Mom is staying but Dad is going away. In our life, Dad was flipping the script. He was staying, Mom was going, and Pamela and I were going with her. Dad said all this was reasonable. "Your mom and I love each other," he claimed, "but we're simply not compatible."

Later I learned that the real reason was that Dad had fallen in love with another woman. At the time, though, neither he nor Mom brought up that issue. My first reaction was to feel protective of Mom. By nature, I'm protective of people I love. I'm not sure about the origins of that instinct, but it's powerful.

"Don't worry, though, Kim, you and your sister will see me," said Dad. "You'll visit me every summer."

A week later, my mother—Edna Earl Mann—Pamela, and I,

along with my parakeet, rabbit, and everything we could cram into our little car, drove to Mill Creek, North Carolina. We lived with Mom's parents in a small country house where the only lock was a hook-and-eye latch on a screen door. From there we moved to a trailer on the same property that my grandparents owned. That situation, though, didn't last long. Fortunately, Mom met a good man, Amos Parker, a home developer whose son, Stephen, was a little younger than me. Amos and Mom fell in love, married, and soon we were all living in a lovely middle-class home that my stepdad had built for us in Newport, a small coastal city. On the whole, I was cool with all this.

Pamela was not. She was furious with our father and for years wouldn't speak to him. Even when he flew us out to visit him during the summer, she was distant and cold. I reacted differently. I was actually intrigued with Dad's new life, and especially his new wife, Phyllis. She was Jewish, the first Jew I had ever met. By then Dad was living in St. Louis where he had developed a nursing home, Mary's Manor. Eventually Dad and Phyllis would have two children of their own, a son Bryce and daughter Hilary.

Phyllis became a huge influence on my life. She introduced me to ballet, and during those summers in St. Louis enrolled me in dance class. She also took me to ballet performances that I found absolutely thrilling. She was a cultured woman with wide interests. She and her sisters had taken ballet and loved the art form. She saw that I had aptitude and did all she could to encourage me. Phyllis changed the course of my life.

It's fascinating to reflect on that fact. I don't remember when I realized that Dad had left Mom for Phyllis. But I had to have known it early on. For some reason, I didn't dwell on that fact. I accepted it. And in doing so, I was able to bond with a woman who had warm feelings for the two daughters her husband had brought to their marriage.

I enjoyed watching Phyllis light candles to welcome in the Sabbath as we gathered at her mom's house every Friday night. Phyllis told me that we both had the same Bible but she believed that Jesus was a prophet, not the Messiah. That was my first introduction to mainstream Jewish faith, practice, and culture.

My own mother was Methodist, as were her parents, and we went to church faithfully every Sunday. My heart belonged to Jesus. I was always inviting friends to Bible study and trying to share my faith.

Back in Newport, I combined my love for ballet with my affinity for baton twirling. I was in the swim of junior—and then senior—high school life. Susan Sledge, a former Miss North Carolina contestant, became another mentor. She ran a dance studio, drove a Corvette, and taught tap, jazz, and ballet. Looking back, I see it as rinky-dink, small-town instruction, but sometimes rinky-dink, small-town instruction is just what a young girl needs. I certainly did. Susan undoubtedly helped me on my way. I was an eager learner, ready to soak up instruction of any kind. I became a head majorette and also acted in and choreographed our high school play, *Once Upon a Mattress*. I was strong in math and science and had the highest average in our school in chemistry. I played flute and piccolo in the band too. I may have been a jack of all trades and master of none, but during my senior year I was voted Most Talented.

This was the seventies, and the centerpiece of my musical culture was Joni Mitchell. Her aesthetic spoke to my heart. I loved the sound of her voice, her guitar, and especially her lyrical poetry. Decades later, I still listen to her *Blue* album on a regular basis. It has never lost its freshness. Growing up on the beaches of the Carolina coast, I took solace singing "Song to a Seagull." (Say that five times fast.) I saw the seagull, as did Joni, "out of reach, out of cry." Joni swept me away. She showed me what it meant to be an artist, a free and female artist. Everything about her was sublime.

During precollege summers, I had a job playing guitar and singing on a four-mast schooner, the *Spanish Main*. I entertained four cruises a day, singing my repertoire of Joni Mitchell, Seals and Crofts, and John Denver songs.

I enrolled at East Carolina University in Greenville because Susan Sledge had gone there. I also continued my summers in St. Louis where I took classes at Washington University in various forms of dance. I was accumulating credits left and right in anything involving movement to music. As a result, I graduated in three years with a BFA in dance. During my college years, I had a boyfriend who majored in acting.

I moved to New York in the summer of 1979 with four other girls from college because we had all landed summer jobs dancing in *The Music Man* at Jones Beach on Long Island. Moving to the mecca of showbusiness with our first professional job elated us.

The mother of one of my roommates got us a safe and secure place to stay in Greenwich Village. The Markle Evangeline Residence, founded by the Salvation Army in the early 1900s, had originally been intended as a temporary residence for women who had come to New York as students, interns, and professionals, but its demographic had apparently changed since its inception. We looked like babes—I mean that literally—compared to the other residents whose average age seemed to be around seventy-five. So much for the temptation for us girls to go wild.

The five of us arrived with the naivete of bright-eyed, small-town girls aspiring to become Broadway stars. We walked the streets laughing and singing like Laverne and Shirley: "Give us any chance we'll take it! . . . We're gonna make our dreams come true!"

I quickly learned, however, that New York was a dangerous city. I was told not to walk around with a smile on my face—my natural demeanor—because that smile could be misconstrued. So I walked around with a scowl. The scowl didn't last long. I'm afraid I'm a natural-born smiler. My solution was to walk really fast and wear a smile all the time. After all, according to Annie, you're never fully dressed without one.

From Markle, the girls and I moved to seedy Times Square where, walking down the street, someone on a high floor dropped a wine bottle that landed a foot in front of me. Welcome to the real world. Then it was on to an apartment on Second Avenue near the UN where a car bomb exploded on our street. By that time my actor boyfriend had moved to New York and we were living together. We were getting along well until he described his recent encounter with Mary Tyler Moore. He was working as a bellman at the Waldorf Towers, a swanky section of the hotel where I first met Glen, where he carried Ms. Moore's bags to her room.

"I'd love to have a sugar mama," he said. "If Mary Tyler Moore ever gave me the green light, I'd be on her like white on rice."

"Is that something you really want to tell me?" I asked.

"You always say you want the truth. Well, that's the truth."

That was also the end of our half-baked romance. He moved back to North Carolina, and I shifted all my focus on getting to work on Broadway.

Then came a break. Frank Wagner, our jazz dance teacher from college, was hired by Disney to choreograph *Snow White and the Seven Dwarfs*. I auditioned along with Lynn Williford—the same Lynn who set me up with Glen—and we were hired. That led to my next job, dancing in a variety show called *America* with the Rockettes at Radio City Music Hall, the show I was doing when I met Glen.

Dancing had always brought me joy and fulfillment before I met Glen. Without him, I felt sad and empty. I had spent three months in anguish, begging God to bring Glen back to me to no avail. Then it suddenly dawned on me. When Jesus was in anguish, he prayed to his father to take his cup of suffering from him but concluded with, "Not my will, but yours be done" (Luke 22:42 NIV).

With that epiphany, I got down on my knees and prayed, "Lord, you know the future and you know what's best for me. I want whatever *you* want for me." Then another scripture came to mind:

> Trust in the LORD with all your heart,
> And lean not on your own understanding;
> In all your ways acknowledge Him,
> And He shall direct your paths.
>
> —PROVERBS 3:5–6 NKJV

Once I placed my trust in God's perfect will for my life, my fears and insecurities melted away. I was no longer depressed, anxious, frustrated, or worried. A wave of peace washed over me. My joy returned. I was excited about what God had in store for me—whatever that might be. I was ready and waiting to be amazed.

Miraculously, the very next day, October 5, 1981, the phone rang. It was Glen.

CHAPTER 4

WHITE FIRS AND PONDEROSA PINES

Those towering trees are what I most remember as the SUV climbed up the snowcapped Sierra Nevada carrying me to Harrah's Lake Tahoe Hotel and Casino.

What was I doing? And why was I doing it?

The easiest answer is the most honest answer and the same answer to which I always revert—love. I was doing it for love.

But I was also doing it out of shock and sympathy. A day earlier, when I heard Glen's voice say, "Kim," I nearly hung up. I figured he'd have a notebook filled with excuses to offer me— and I wanted to hear none of them. I had been hurt badly enough and, not having a masochistic bone in my body, had no desire to be hurt again. What he said, though, had nothing to do with excuses. His first words took my breath away.

"Jud Strunk is dead."

Glen's voice sounded shaky. He was crying.

"What happened?" I asked. "Was it the plane?"

"He was in the plane, but it wasn't the plane. It was a heart attack. Jud's heart gave out just as he was taking off in a little airport up in Maine. He and his passenger, another buddy, Richard Ayotte, were killed instantly. I can't believe it, Kim. I really can't believe it."

When he began sobbing, I didn't know what to do. All I could say was that I was terribly sorry. I had only met Jud once, but that was enough to realize that he was a great guy.

"It's hard for me to be alone, Kim. I need you with me. I need you right now."

"Where are you, Glen?"

"Lake Tahoe. Can't stop thinking about Jud and Richard. They were my age. Forty-five. Their whole life in front of them. Why? I keep asking myself why. It's hard for me to be alone right now, Kim. It really is. There's no one I want to be with except you."

"Look, Glen, my heart is with you, but you have to know that you broke my heart. This is the first time you've called in three months. And then all that business with Tanya."

"That business is over. It was crazy. One last fling of madness."

"But is it true? Did it happen? Or did the tabloids make it up?"

"The tabloids blew it up, but, yes, it was true. I went back to her but the same way a dope fiend goes back to the crack den."

"So you're blaming it all on her."

"No, baby, I'm blaming myself. I'm as bad as her. Together, we're double trouble. There are no two people in the world less suited for each other than me and Tanya. Just like there are no two people in the world better suited for each other than you and me. I promise you that. Promise you with all my heart."

I remained silent for a good minute. Maybe the longest minute of my life. I wanted to doubt him. I wanted to believe him. I wanted to believe him more than I wanted to doubt him, but I also wanted to protect myself. I needed to be guarded, cautious, wary. I'd be a fool to be anything but. Mainly I needed time to think. I had to admit it: I was excited to hear from him. But I was also devastated to hear about Jud. I tried to understand the connection between these two events: Jud's death and Glen's call. I couldn't and didn't believe that Glen was using the tragedy to win me back. My deepest belief was Glen was truly devastated. He had to be. And he had to be sincere in calling me for comfort. I had to be flattered. I had to respond. I had to get on a plane and go to him.

So I did. Of course, it was easy because Glen's people made the arrangements. All I had to do was pack a bag. But packing that bag was without doubt a huge act of faith. Packing that bag meant leaving my New York life behind and following Glen, no matter where that might lead.

I think now of the words from the book of Ruth where she says, "Wherever you go, I will go; and where you lodge, I will lodge; your people shall be my people, and your God, my God" (1:16). Ruth was not speaking to a man, but to Naomi, her widowed mother-in-law who was returning to Israel. Ruth was more than willing to follow; she was compelled. She sensed it was God's will, not hers, to make the trip. It was in Israel that she and Naomi, both impoverished, found protection in Boaz, who eventually married Ruth. Their son, Obed, became the grandfather of King David and an ancestor of Jesus.

The story comes to mind because, thinking back, I had something of that same feeling. I was more than willing to follow what seemed to be my destiny; I felt compelled. That's the only way I can explain doing what would otherwise seem slightly insane. Why else rejoin a man who had not only spurned me but indulged in a madcap fling with a former lover? Ruth's statement resonates in my heart because it speaks of loyalty and devotion. Loyalty and devotion, in spite of an avalanche of obstacles, were critical forces in bringing me back to Glen. Both forces were defined and driven by love. I may have been too young to have seen it then, but I certainly see it now. Love, loyalty, and devotion are what sustained our relationship. Without those three essential elements, I would not have packed my bag, and this story would end right here.

But gloriously—and also dangerously—the story continued. I flew to Tahoe. I took in the awesome beauty of that mountain range. I arrived at Harrah's Casino and was brought to Glen's penthouse suite. He was there to greet me. He swept me up into his arms and held me like he would never let me go and kissed me like he never wanted it to end. After three months of agony, praying, and waiting, I felt like I had my answer from God.

The chef had prepared a candlelight dinner. Filet mignon. Dom Pérignon. Tiramisu. After dinner Glen asked me to dance to soft, lilting guitar music flowing from the stereo.

"Is that something you recorded?" I asked.

"Something I wrote for you. It's not beautiful enough to really capture you, but at least I tried."

He held me closer, looked into my eyes, and said, "You look different, Kim. I'm seeing something I haven't seen before."

"What do you mean?"

"You seem peaceful."

"I didn't seem that way before?" I asked.

"You seemed intimidated by me—and maybe by my world."

"I was intimidated at first, but I'm not anymore."

"Why?" he wanted to know.

"When you called and asked me here, I obviously had to make a decision. My first reaction was to tell you off—"

"Well, you kind of did—"

"But not for long."

"I got off easy. I still feel terrible about how I treated you."

"Your apology wasn't what got me here," I said.

"Then what was it?"

"Trusting God. I've simply decided to trust God with my life. I'm here because my spirit is telling me this is where I belong."

"My spirit and your spirit," said Glen, "are saying the same thing."

Our words fell away, and we danced to the softly swaying music he had made for me. The music was seductive, but, then again, everything about Glen was seductive. He drew me—just as he had drawn the world—to his ineffable charm.

I already knew that I would no longer resist. I desired him as much as he desired me. We danced our way into the bedroom. Our physical connection was nothing less than phenomenal.

The phenomenon, though, although thrillingly sexual, was reinforced by the very spirit we had mentioned. Yes, our bodies made love and the feeling was divine, but it was our spirits that made love, our spirits that allowed tenderness and sensitivity to prevail, our spirits that were satiated in a way I had never experienced before.

In the afterglow, with the guitar music soothing our excitement and the stars twinkling between the white firs and ponderosa pine trees towering outside the wraparound windows, we fell into peaceful slumber.

We slept till noon, maybe later.

"You gotta tell me what you dreamed about," said Glen.

"I dreamed about you."

"Was I being good, or was I on a wild tear?"

"You were playing your guitar," I said. "You were singing to me."

"Wasn't no dream, baby," said Glen. "I got up in the middle of the night and did just that."

The day was sunny and glorious. Glen learned I'd never been west of St. Louis, and laughed.

"Well, today I'll show you Lake Tahoe, and one day I'll show you California."

I nodded eagerly, thinking of Hollywood, Los Angeles, San Francisco, and the Pacific Ocean. I was still daydreaming about California when Glen said abruptly, "Get your coat. We're going for a walk."

We walked outside of Harrah's and crossed the street. Then Glen spun me around and proudly proclaimed, "I just want you to know that I am a man of my word. I said I'd take you to California, and now you're in California." Our hotel was located on a street called Stateline, so by leading me across the street, Glen had literally taken me into California. He smiled and pulled me close in a giant bear hug. "I'm going to enjoy showing you the world!"

I did see the world, and I did leave my old world behind. I left my job in New York. In fact, I left New York altogether. From that moment on, I stayed with Glen. I believed that his commitment to me was inviolable, just as inviolable as my commitment to him.

I was back in the whirlwind, and I was loving it. I went to his show every night and quickly learned the ropes. The preshow flurry of activity simulated the synchronization of a NASCAR pit stop: Race through the bowels of the casino and kitchen where, no matter how great the hurry, Glen stops to greet every last cook, waiter, and dishwasher. Whisper to me, "Welcome to the back roads by the rivers of my memory." Arrive in the dressing room. Autograph a pile of photos. Meet the local mayor. Meet the local councilman. Meet the local president of the Glen Campbell fan club. Sit down for a series of quick interviews. Get outfitted by the valet. Get made up by the makeup lady. Review the set list. Insert last-minute changes. Take out that song. Put in this song. And then go out there and kill it. Glen always killed it.

Afterward, the dressing room was like Grand Central. Well-wishers by the dozens, but well-wishers like Dean Martin or Ray Charles or Frank Sinatra or Dick Van Dyke. If I sat in the corner to watch, Glen came to get me, put his arm around me, and included me in every picture.

"This is my angel," he said, "and I want the world to know it."

All good except for one thing. That one thing can be best expressed by a rider in Glen's contract that stipulated his dressing room must be equipped with a full bar. That rider was an omen that, in the late fall of 1981, I did not fully understand. Of course I remembered how he'd gotten sloppy drunk the first night we met, but I wrote that off as an anomaly. It wasn't. After every show, he hit the bottle and hit it hard. He went from sweet and humble Glen to belligerent and self-centered Glen. My first thought was to protect him from himself by showing how much I loved the gentle Glen and ignored the grumpy Glen. I was determined that "Gentle on My Mind" transform from a simple song to a permanent way of life.

My determination was hampered by endless challenges, the most important of which I was not aware. Glen was an alcoholic, and alcoholism, I did not yet realize, is a disease. It isn't caused by lack of willpower. It's a result of a lethal combination of biochemistry but also emotional history. There was so much about Glen's physical and psychological past that I just didn't know.

Like many entertainers, he had the sleeping habits of a vampire. He duct-taped the edges of his bedroom blackout drapery to the wall, keeping all light out. He often slept till four in the afternoon. Sometimes drinking was restricted to after the show, but most of the time it began beforehand. The drinking never really stopped.

So I decided I would stop. I would set the example. Though drinking was never a problem for me, I had shared wine with him. No more. I wanted Glen to see that you can celebrate life without being buzzed.

"I hope my decision doesn't upset you," I said.

"Not at all, angel. Makes me happy. Happy to see that you have a mind of your own."

My plan—that my mind would influence his—went awry. Once I stopped, he seemed to drink even more. I didn't use the word *enable* then—I was hardly that sophisticated—but that's what I was doing. Without saying it, I implied that, although I would no longer drink, I had no objections to his drinking. Well, I did have objections, and at what I considered the right time I voiced those objections. But my voice was drowned out by the excitement of his superstar lifestyle. If he said anything, it was something like, "It isn't a problem, honey. I've got it all under control."

Denial was another term with which I was not familiar. Not yet anyway. He was in denial, and to a great degree I was as well. But neither of us could deny or resist the glamour of the fast-moving life we were living. So after a show if he got too drunk and could barely walk, he leaned on me. I fell into the role of caregiver, a role that I maintained for the rest of our relationship. I am glad for that role, I am ambivalent about that role, I have a thousand conflicting thoughts about that role, but it is finally a role I came to accept. Early on, I saw that someone needed to save this man from himself. The ultimate Savior is God, but when it comes to saving loved ones who are inextricable parts of our lives, God works in mysterious ways.

Meanwhile, the pace picked up. We were off to Africa, where Glen teed off at the first Million Dollar Challenge at the Gary Player Country Club in newly completed Sun City resort in Bophuthatswana. I met Sean Connery. I met Telly Savalas. I met Johnny Mathis. I met Joe DiMaggio. The red carpet seemed five miles long. There were famous people everywhere I looked. We had our own security detail. Glen won more money at baccarat that week than I made at Radio City in a year. Radio City was history. History-making stars were our dinner guests. Manicures in the morning. Massages in the afternoon. Who lived like this? Glen did. I did. Even though I'd stuck to my pledge and never touched a drink, I was high. High on the high life. High on love. High on Glen.

Glen loved golf and wanted to teach me all about it so I could enjoy the event. He told me that none other than Jack Nicklaus was there.

"I didn't know he plays golf," I said.

"What!" Glen exclaimed. "He's probably the greatest golfer in the world."

"Really? I knew he was a great actor, and I loved him in *One Flew Over the Cuckoo's Nest*, but I didn't know he plays golf."

"That's Jack Nicholson. This is Jack Nicklaus."

I was flunking sport quizzes left and right, but Glen didn't seem to mind. He kept saying how much he loved me, how grateful he was for my presence, how he wanted to be with me every minute of every day.

"Even on the golf course?"

"That's the only exception."

The next day it rained and, leaving the grandstand, I struggled to negotiate a big puddle of water only to be swept up by actor Ernest Borgnine, who carried me over to where Glen had finished the eighteenth hole.

"Special delivery," said Borgnine.

"Special lady," said Glen as he took me into his arms.

He was carrying me and I was thrilled being carried, thrilled to be on this wondrous ride. We went from South Africa to Fort Worth to do a show with Rita Coolidge. We stayed with Glen's sister and her husband Ed. Sweet sister Sandy was ten years my senior and bore a striking resemblance to Glen.

"When Sandy took me home to Arkansas," said Ed, "her brothers looked like giants to me. JW, standing at six feet four, was nicknamed Shorty only because he was shorter than the others. Gerald, the tallest, picked me up off the floor and said, 'Hey, Shorty. Look what Sandy brought us home to play with!'" Ed said his feet hit the ground running, all the way back to Texas.

Ed and Sandy welcomed me with open arms. Like the rest of his siblings, Sandy had a beautiful singing voice. Sandy sang "Try A Little Kindness" with Glen in the show. Their genetic harmony was not just audible. As they sang together, you could feel the familial harmony of love. Rita Coolidge, who had dueted with Glen on "Somethin' 'Bout You Baby I Like," opened the show.

Next day Rita and her gang joined us for Thanksgiving at Sandy and Ed's. Talk about gratitude! The meal was bountiful. My heart was bountiful. Life was good.

"Life can be tricky," sister Sandy said to me that evening before we left. Her tone wasn't ominous, but it was definitely serious. I wasn't sure what she meant.

"I've been worried about my brother, but now that he's met you, Kim, I'm a lot less worried."

I encouraged her to speak her mind. She talked about Glen's drinking. "All it takes is one drink," she said, "and then something snaps. I don't know what that 'snap' is all about, but I'm praying for him. And I'm gonna start praying for you."

I heard what Sandy said, and of course I knew it to be true. I'd seen it with my own eyes. Knowing that Sandy and Ed were committed to praying for us gave me confidence that God was at work.

Believe it or not, the next day we headed back to South Africa to do a show. Glen had a show with the Beach Boys, whom I'd never seen live. Having spent a good deal of my childhood in the North Carolina surfing community of Atlantic Beach, I grew up on the Beach Boys. I loved them.

On the trip over, Glen couldn't stop telling Beach Boys stories. He said that playing bass guitar while singing the high part on "She's a Little Old Lady from Pasadena" was "like rubbin' your belly and pattin' your head at the same time." He described Brian's phenomenal ability to compose and structure harmonies. He credited Brian as one of the great masters with whom he had been privileged to play. In 1964, when Brian was unable to tour, he named Glen as his replacement. When Jimmy Webb had first told me how Glen had substituted for Brian, Glen shrugged it off as no big deal. But on this plane ride back to the other side of the world, he was in a mood to reminisce.

"Touring with the Beach Boys," he said, "was my first taste of big-time show biz. I love music fans, and especially female music fans, but some of those gals can get awfully aggressive. Wasn't used to having women chase me down and tear off my clothes. That's when I understood that being a star can also be a little scary. After the tour, I was glad to be back in the studio.

I loved playing with the Wrecking Crew. We were so in demand, sometimes we played three different sessions a day."

"Wrecking Crew?" I said, puzzled.

"Before us, studio musicians would dress proper. We wouldn't. Me and, say, Leon Russell, who was an ace piano player, and Carol Kaye, a killer on bass and Hal Blaine on drums . . . well, the four of us strolled into the studio wearing whatever we wanted. Jeans and T-shirts. We didn't care 'cause we knew we could play. Some of those old-time producers claimed our casual ways were gonna wreck the music business. That's how we became the Wrecking Crew. But the music business is built on hits, and we had what it took to turn out hits. Guys who were really in the know—like Phil Spector and Brian Wilson—couldn't care less how we dressed. They used us every chance they could. I'd be playing four, five, six sessions a day. That was a lot more fun than those crazy thirty-city tours. I was making double and triple overtime. After what I'd been through before landing in LA, I was in hog heaven."

"What had you been through?" I asked.

"Baby," he said, "that's a story for another day."

Meeting the Beach Boys in Bophuthatswana was a thrill, but an even bigger thrill was a video tape a fan gave Glen after the show. In the pre-YouTube world, to get a chance to see Glen performing on a 1965 *Shindig!* TV episode was a rare treat. Glen and I watched it together. I stared at it in wonderment.

Twenty-nine-year-old Glen sang this haunting song written by Brian Wilson ironically titled "Guess I'm Dumb." Brian believed in Glen's talent as a solo artist and wrote the song specifically for him. There's absolutely nothing dumb about the song, the singer, or the singer's performance. The story is about a young man who has lost a love he treasured. The source of his distress is his inability to let go of a love that may never be realized. Glen sings many of the phrases in falsetto.

"I think I was trying to sound like Roy Orbison," he said jokingly.

"You sound like yourself," I said. "You sound so sincere."

"I was sincere," Glen agreed. "When I look back at those run-ins I had with women, I was dumb."

"Let's not talk," I said. "Let's just listen."

When the song was over, I asked him to rewind the tape so I could watch it again. There was something ethereal about it, something otherworldly. It was more than Glen appearing young and handsome. He sang it as if he had lived it. Was he just a good performer, or was this absolute proof that the man whom I so deeply loved had remarkable depth? I sensed his depth was rooted in pain. "Guess I'm Dumb" is a song drowning in pain.

That night was the first time he spoke to me about his first wife, Diane.

"I was in Albuquerque, playing in my uncle's band. Uncle Dick knew a woman who came to the shows and always brought her teenaged daughter. Now keep in mind, Uncle Dick was hardly my favorite uncle. That requires an explanation. See, it was my Uncle Boo who first took me from Delight, Arkansas, to Casper, Wyoming, where we tried to make it as musicians. We played all sorts of buckets of blood, roadhouses with sawdust on the floor, even homes of ill repute. But it didn't work. We were so broke we didn't have enough money to buy a bus ticket back home. My dad was even broker and said to ask his sister's husband, my uncle Dick, for some money. Uncle Dick couldn't have cared less. 'Keep digging them ditches,' he said, 'and pay your own fare back home.' It was only a few years later when Dick realized

I had talent and called me to join his band. I almost didn't do it 'cause I was still mad at how he'd treated me and Boo. I was also scared he might leave me stranded if his band ever went bust. But desperate men will do desperate things. And besides, I wasn't even a man. I was a teenager chasing a dream that my guitar was my ticket to freedom. So I went. And there I was at the Chesterfield Club in New Mexico when Uncle Dick said his lady friend wanted me to meet her daughter. *Sure thing, Uncle Dick. Diane, meet Glen.* Diane was pretty, and Diane was eager to have sex. I hadn't had sex before, but I sure had been thinking about it. I sneaked her into my motel room. We loved it up real good. My daddy had told me how babies are made but nothing 'bout how to prevent making 'em. Didn't think twice about it till Diane turned up pregnant. I was eighteen, she was fifteen. I felt like the world's worst sinner. I also knew I had to do the right thing and marry Diane. Diane's mom went berserk and said she couldn't move in the motel with me. She couldn't marry me. She was out of my life. Except she wasn't. She went against her mom and married me anyway. Her mom wouldn't even come to the courthouse. It was only me, Diane, and her dad. I found a tiny one-bedroom apartment on the wrong side of the tracks. We couldn't even afford curtains. We lived on canned soup. We got rid of the roaches but not the rats. Watching Diane's belly get bigger, I got scared. Couldn't afford a crib, couldn't even afford diapers. Uncle Dick's band was playing less gigs and Uncle Dick wasn't about to loan me a dime.

"By the time the baby was born, I was a mental case. But when I saw my son, Glen Travis Campbell Jr., I was happier than I'd ever been. Busting with pride. That little baby was the most beautiful thing I ever did lay my eyes on. And then . . ."

Glen stopped talking. I could tell he was fighting back tears. I drew closer to him and urged him to continue. He bit his lip and said, "My son never left the hospital alive. He died after two days. His lungs never developed. Diane's dad paid for the funeral because I didn't have the money. I'd been raised a strict Christian, and I've always believed in God, but the way I was raised had me believing God was punishing me. I'd had sex before marriage. I'd sinned. And there was no one to comfort me. I was a thousand miles away from home. Didn't even call Daddy or Mama to tell them. Was too heartbroken. Too ashamed.

"If I'd been a wiser man instead of a green kid, I would have known our marriage was over. We tried to make it work, but the death of our baby hung over our heads like a dark cloud. Diane got closer to her mom. Because her mom never did like me, I felt that same disapproval coming from Diane. Nothing I did was right. But Diane got pregnant again and in 1956 our daughter Debby was born. In the winter of 1957, I had family living in Houston and wanted to take Diane and Debby there to celebrate Christmas. Diane refused. 'Take Debby,' she said. 'I'll stay here.' So I drove my sixteen-month-old baby in a sixteen-year-old car down to Texas. Well, if Diane didn't want to come to Houston, I figured she'd wouldn't want to come to Arkansas to meet Mama and Daddy. But she finally agreed. Taking her wasn't a good idea, 'cause when we finally arrived she refused to go inside the house to meet my family. She stayed in the car and kept honking the horn for me to come out. I was mortified, but what could I do? I apologized for my wife's behavior. My folks were so kind they didn't even get mad. When we got back to Albuquerque, it was a policeman pal that set me straight.

"'Look, Glen,' he said, 'I hate to be the one to bring you the bad news, but if I don't tell you someone else will. I believe it's better for you to hear it from a friend.'

"'What are you talking about, man?'

"'Your wife.'

"'What about my wife?'

"'She done found someone else.'

"I didn't want to believe it. I had to ask, 'How do you know all this?'

"'Seen it with my own eyes, Glen. Was on patrol. Came up on a car that was illegally parked. Looked inside and don't need to tell you what I saw going on in the back seat. I looked the other way and just left the parking citation on the windshield.'

"I was shocked. Stayed shocked for days until I finally did what I knew had to be done. I confronted Diane. She denied it. But I was prepared. That's why I asked my pal to give me the parking citation. I showed it to her. Told her what he had seen. She admitted it. I flew into a rage. I pushed her against the wall. Had my hands around her neck but God intervened. God said, *Leave this woman alone. Do not choke her. Do not strike her. Let her go.* Thanking God, I let her go. Next morning, she went off with baby Debby. Lost my son. Lost my wife. Lost my daughter. 'Guess I'm Dumb' should've been my theme song instead of 'Rhinestone Cowboy.'"

When Glen opened up like that, as he increasingly did, I came to love him even more. I came to understand him in new ways. The betrayal, loss, and financial struggles of his past stood in stark contrast to the love, intimacy, and outlandish comfort we now shared. In Africa, for example, our hosts had a private jet take us to Zululand for a camera safari. We were greeted by native dancers dressed—or undressed if you will—in traditional garb to welcome us. I'd done a bit of African dance with the Rockettes, but this was the real thing.

We slept in luxurious grass huts that had been refitted with thatched ceilings and massive wooden beams. Our room was appointed with sculptures and artifacts from the ancient Zulu culture. The wicker blades of a large ceiling fan circulated the hot summer air as we made love to the cries of wild animals and basked in the sultry afterglow of our first night in the jungle. The exotic setting seemed to soothe my savage beast.

We had breakfast in the jungle and then the safari—the bucks, zebras, antelopes, and baboons all roaming freely. We were taken to visit a cheetah who'd been rescued as a cub and raised in the backyard of a game preservationist. The animal lived in a chain-linked enclosure. We were told it was safe to get up close. We were inches away from her piercing, unblinking eyes reflecting the gold of the afternoon sun. I was nervous. I wasn't sure that, no matter how tame, the cheetah wouldn't decide to have us both for lunch. But I stayed, and I stared, and Glen and I praised God for the beauty of his creatures.

The final night was the most enchanting. We sat around a campfire. Glen brought out his guitar. Everyone—drivers, cooks, repairmen, little children, and elderly villagers—gathered around. Glen sang church hymns from his childhood and then went on to sing some of his favorite country classics—"Mama Tried," "Make the World Go Away," "I'm So Lonesome I Could Cry." And even though these were songs written for a culture foreign from the audience listening that night, it made no difference. Tears flowed from the faces of these people. They heard Glen's heart. He touched theirs. And I, the young woman that I was, witnessed utter magic. I witnessed the universality of music.

CHAPTER 5

BY THE TIME WE GOT TO PHOENIX

We had met in May. It was now December. So much had happened so quickly. Glen was taking me to Phoenix to see the house he had just bought. He confided to me that after living in LA for more than twenty years, he wanted to get away from the ex-wives and bad memories. He bought the house on a whim, had his belongings shipped, but had not yet slept there. Phoenix represented a fresh start in life for Glen, and he couldn't wait to show me the house.

The property was enormous. The approach, lined with olive trees, offset a five-acre grove of orange, grapefruit, and lemon trees. A cobblestone driveway passed through wrought iron entry gates where, in the circular motor court, Glen's cream-colored Rolls-Royce Corniche convertible stood, top down to show off the cranberry leather seats. The house itself, a Spanish hacienda spanning nearly eight thousand square feet, sat on two highly manicured acres shaded by four dozen palm trees. I walked up the front steps through a series of arches into a regal courtyard filled with birds of paradise. A traditional Spanish fountain sat in the midst of it all. Fuchsia bougainvillea exploded against the white stucco walls. Gardenia and orange blossoms—a sweet heady fragrance filled the air. The tall, arched entry doors, made of glass and iron, were adorned with baskets of sculpted roses.

Beaming with joy and a giddy, childlike enthusiasm, Glen led me inside, through the grand entry, and then into an enormous great room. Its exposed trestle ceiling glowed with the light of four large chandeliers. The space spanned forty-eight feet from its grand fireplace at the eastern end to a gourmet kitchen at the western end that would have made Martha Stewart swoon. Along with a comfortable seating area, the room contained Glen's pride and joy, an antique pool table inlaid with extensive marquetry of exotic woods, and a Yamaha grand piano handpicked for him by Jimmy Webb.

The rest of the rooms were of equal scale and character. There were San Carlos tiled floors and heavy solid doors throughout. Glen had purchased all the custom-made furniture with the house. Its oversized, ornately carved mahogany beds, tables, chairs, and the large oriental rugs made me feel like I was inside a lavish old-world estate.

The backyard was landscaped with formal rose gardens and tiled planters. There was an outdoor kitchen, outdoor fireplace, and a tiled pool shaped like a Van Cleef & Arpels Alhambra.

Glen saved the master bedroom for last. To enter, we walked through french doors. The space was enormous. The centerpiece was a huge mahogany four-poster bed with a headboard filled with elaborately carved birds, butterflies, and fleur-de-lis. A matching twelve-foot-long, nine-foot-high armoire anchored the other side of the room.

"It's a palace," I said.

"It's yours," he said.

"Not exactly."

"Yes, exactly. I want to live here with you. I want you to marry me. What do you say?"

I said yes, not once but twenty times over. I couldn't stop saying yes. Couldn't stop feeling that this was the most wonderful moment of my life. No hesitation. No concern. Simply *yes, yes, yes*.

To show his consideration, Glen's first concern was meeting my folks. He wanted to assure them of his sincerity. He wanted to see where I'd grown up and spend Christmas with me in North Carolina. My mother, Edna, and my stepdad, Amos, were thrilled. So were my sister Pam and step-brother Stephen. In fact, the whole town was thrilled. Wherever we walked, people gawked. Glen never failed to stop and greet a stranger, sign an autograph, have his picture taken. Like most true entertainers, Glen thrived on attention. But unlike many entertainers, he thrived just as much on lavishing attention on others. My parents were crazy about him. He came with us to the Christmas Eve service at Saint James United Methodist, the church where I'd been raised to love the Lord. When the minister asked Glen to sing, I was embarrassed. Glen wasn't. He went right up to the pulpit and said, "I'm the seventh son of eight boys and four girls. Mama went to church every Sunday. Because we were all breastfed, we went to church with her. So my first memories are of church, and I feel very blessed being in this beautiful church sanctuary with all of you on this sacred night."

He then sang "The Lord's Prayer."

Next Glen wanted me to see his humble origins and to meet his huge family, so we flew to Arkansas for New Years. His family reveled in telling stories about their earlier days as poor sharecroppers and how they spent portions of their summers picking tomatoes in Indiana as migrant workers. Glen remembered shivering through the nights in tomato-field huts with no food except, of course, tomatoes.

Glen loved to joke about the austerity of his childhood. He

used to say, "We were so poor we couldn't afford electricity, so we had to watch TV by candlelight."

Glen's father, John Wesley Campbell (Wes), was a hardworking man who struggled to provide for his family. His first wife passed away, leaving him with two sons, Wayne and Lindell. Then Wes married Carrie Dell Stone, a tall, statuesque woman with steel-blue eyes and a strong, square chin. She gave birth to ten children, including two sets of twins with only one surviving from each set. In good times, Carrie cooked one hundred biscuits every morning to feed her brood before the entire family went out into the fields to pick cotton. In bad times they went without breakfast and ate anything they could catch, including opossum and squirrels. Carrie would breastfeed her youngest and then pull the baby behind her on a cotton sack while she worked in the fields. At times the heat and work were so intense Carrie would pass out.

The six Campbell brothers, their cousins, and kin were all fun-loving pranksters. On one occasion, a game of cowboys and Indians ended up with Glen's brother Ronald accidentally getting shot with a BB gun and Glen getting stabbed in the butt with a pocketknife. Glen's grandfather took pleasure in inviting kids to feel his soft tooth, then after giving them a good hard "bite," he warned them, "Always remember, kids, there ain't no such thing as a soft tooth!" This was how they were taught lessons and how they had fun. As Glen explained, "There wasn't a whole lot to do back on the farm."

They told me the miraculous story of how Glen's life had been spared when he was just a toddler. Carrie asked Glen's older brother Ronald to keep an eye on Glen on the porch. Ronald himself was just a child and had not noticed that Glen had wandered off. When their mother returned, she didn't see Glen.

"Ronald, where's Glen?"

"I don't know," Ronald said. "He was here just a minute ago."

A wave of panic rolled over Carrie. She rushed toward the creek that ran behind the house. Her eyes frantically searched the banks as she called out for Glen. Then she saw a little foot caught in the crook of a branch and Glen's body completely submerged in the murky water. She reached down and pulled him out, but she was too late. Glen had stopped breathing and had already turned blue. Carrie began screaming hysterically. Glen's older brother Lindell had just returned home from military boot camp where he had received training in CPR. Hearing his stepmother's cries, he ran to her as fast as he could.

"He's not breathing! He's not breathing!" she shouted.

Lindell grabbed the baby from her arms and held him upside down. As he pounded Glen's back, gray sludge began oozing from his small, fragile lungs. Then he laid the child on the ground, placed his mouth over Glen's nose and mouth, and began filling Glen's lungs with air. He continued mouth-to-mouth as the family gathered around, crying and praying, "Dear Jesus, bring Glen back! Please, Jesus! Please!" Suddenly Glen began to breathe on his own. Tears of sorrow turned to tears of joy. There were no local doctors or hospitals, so the family merely took Glen up to the house, wrapped him in blankets, and kept him under their observation. That night, they were all amazed to see Glen keeping time with the music on the radio. They all believed that God had spared Glen's life for a reason.

The whole family sang and played instruments. As time went on, though, it was clear that Glen's talent was special. By age five, he was already proficient on guitar and wanted one of his own. Carrie worked in the fields to earn enough money, five dollars to be exact, to buy Glen a child-sized guitar from Sears. Wes's brother, Uncle Boo, was a little older than Glen and is credited with helping Glen learn to play guitar. Glen said he threatened to pinch his pinky finger off with a pair of pliers if he didn't use it on the fingerboard.

Glen liked to say that he was born during the Great Depression, when poor people living in the city stood in breadlines and went to soup kitchens. Then he'd add, "We didn't have those luxuries in the rural South."

Delight, Arkansas, had a population of less than three hundred when Glen was a kid. It had one church and two country stores. Suddenly the tone became somber as the family began to disclose just how hard it was to survive back then. One winter when Wes became convinced that he couldn't feed his family, he went to the woods, put a shotgun to his head, and was about to commit suicide when he saw a squirrel run up a tree. He shot the squirrel. Then he saw a second, a third, and finally there were nearly a dozen. He shot them all. Those squirrels became dinner, and Wes put thoughts of suicide aside—at least for a while.

On another day—when Glen was six—Wes's despondency returned. There wasn't a morsel of food in their cabin.

"Will one of you boys take that gun over there and just shoot me?" said Wes.

Gerald was horrified and pleaded, "Oh, Daddy, don't talk like that! Please, Daddy, please!"

Shorty took a different approach. Nonchalantly, he said, "I'll do it, Daddy."

Shorty was only about ten years old at the time but had already earned a reputation as a sharpshooter. He picked up the gun, took aim, and shot Wes's hat clean off his head.

Wes jumped up and started screaming, "What are you trying to do? Kill me?"

Shorty responded, "You said that's what you wanted, Daddy!"

"Well, I didn't mean it!" Wes exclaimed. Of course, Shorty had no intention of killing his father.

I thought the story was apocryphal, but every family member swore it was true.

Every last family member embraced me. These were among the sweetest people I'd ever met. I was amazed by their cheerful disposition. After hearing some of the stories about their abject poverty, I presumed that rough life would have taken its toll. But being with them, it was all hugs and kisses. No one seemed to have suffered trauma. And yet . . .

Glen and I awoke late New Year's Day. He asked if I'd like to take a walk through the countryside. It was a cold and gray January afternoon. The barren landscape gave me an uneasy feeling. The leafless trees looked like ghosts. I had a feeling Glen was remembering some ghosts from his past. My feeling turned out to be right.

I started off on a cheerful note. "You have a beautiful family."

"Man, do I ever! Best people in the world."

"I love how they love to laugh."

"Me too," said Glen. "Laughing's always the best medicine."

"Hearing those stories, seems like your childhood wasn't all that bad."

"Well, angel, truth is, I do have some bad memories."

He slowed down the pace of our walk and suddenly turned reflective. "I ever tell you the story about the kittens?"

"No."

"Wanna hear it?'

"I want to hear everything about you."

"Well, we're about to pass by the river where it happened."

Glen sat down on a log in a clearing by the riverbank. I sat next to him. He sighed before he began to speak.

"It's all about these kittens."

"Kittens are always so cute," I said.

"That was the problem. Our cat had the cutest kittens you've ever seen. They were tiny little creatures—every color you can imagine. Must have been six or seven of 'em. I'd watched them being born and felt like they were gifts from God. And then Daddy said, 'Take 'em out and kill 'em.'

"I couldn't believe it. 'What!' I cried. 'Why do you want 'em killed?' I asked.

"''Cause they're gonna want food, and we ain't got no food.'

"'Their mama's gonna feed 'em.'

"'Their mama's gotta stay busy chasing down mice and rats. We don't got room for no kittens. Put 'em in a sack, tie 'em up, and throw them critters in the river.'

"'I can't.'

"''Ain't asking you. I'm telling you. Now *git*!'

"My daddy is a big, strong man. I'd seen him beat some of my brothers to where my mama started crying and begged him to stop. That's how it was back then. That's how you learned discipline. We all knew Daddy loved us, but we all also knew if we disobeyed him we'd get a beating. I knew if I didn't drown those kittens he'd whip me so bad I wouldn't be able to walk for a week. Plus, Kim, you gotta remember—I was his youngest son, and we had this bond. I was raised up to obey him, no matter what. So, sure enough, I kissed each one goodbye and put them squirmy little kittens in a burlap sack, tied it up, and walked to this very river where we're sitting. I took that sack and drew back my arm to throw it in the river but then I pulled back. I just couldn't do it. I was seven years old, Kim, and I was crying like a newborn baby. I was bawling. It broke my little heart. I . . . I . . ."

Glen took my hand, squeezed it hard. His eyes welled up like he was fighting back tears. For a moment I felt as if I was holding hands with that seven-year-old little boy.

"I tried a second time," he said as he wiped back a tear, "and still couldn't do it. But I thought of how Daddy would tear me up and I was just plain scared to go against him. So on the third try I let the sack go, watched it hit the water and then sink on down. I nearly jumped in to save those little kittens, but I didn't. I stayed on the riverbank and must have cried another half hour. Never did do anything so hard in all my life.

"Now I understand why we were raised tough. Daddy taught us to survive. He'd row us out onto that river, to the deepest part, throw us in, and yell, 'Swim!' The swimming part was easy. The hard part was getting out of that sack."

He laughed, attempting to lighten the mood. "I'm just kidding about the sack," he said. "But Daddy really did just throw us in. That's how I learned to swim. Dad made us eat turtles and eels 'cause that's all the food he could find. He showed us how to make money by picking four hundred pounds of cotton—by hand. That earned him four dollars. He taught me to cut a hog's throat. He said, 'Slice the skin from the carcass, scrape the waste from the meat, cut it into pieces, and carry it in to Mama so she can cook it up.' I obeyed. I always obeyed. I killed my share of hogs, but drowning them kittens, Kim, that did something to me. They trusted me, and I threw them in the river."

I was about to say something when Glen stopped me.

"I'm not looking for pity. I'm not blaming no one. I do believe I was raised right. I learned about work, and work is what got me through. Work is what got me all these beautiful things in life."

"You didn't have to work to get me," I said.

That brought out one of those irresistible Glen smiles.

"The heck I didn't," he said. "I had to beg to get you back. Begging's hard work."

"Well, now that I'm here, I'm not going anywhere."

"That's why I love you, angel. You're the first woman I've ever truly trusted."

"In spite of everything, it sounds like you trusted your dad."

"Combination of trust and fear. Did I ever tell you about the boxing match between him and my brother Wayne?"

"No."

"It's a good one, Kim. When we were little and gave Daddy any grief, he brought out his belt. It was the kind of belt that left welts that would burn for days. Then when we got older and started going after each other, like brothers do, he handed us some boxing gloves and told us to fight it out. Came the day my brother Wayne turned eighteen. He'd been schooled at a military camp that was part of the government's antipoverty program during the Great Depression. Wayne built up his body and was strong as an ox. Well, one day Daddy told him to tie up the horses and hook 'em to the wagon. We often rode in a horse-drawn wagon to church. Wayne refused. 'I'm a man now,' he said. 'Get one of the boys to do it.' Wayne's refusal shocked the whole family. No one refused Daddy. Daddy was a man of few words. That day he used no words. He just walked inside and grabbed the gloves. He kept one pair and handed the second one to Wayne. The whole family ran outside to watch. The whole family was afraid that

Wayne would pulverize Daddy. The two stood face-to-face. Both expressionless. No one blinked.

"'The first move is yours,' Daddy said.

"Wayne led with his left. Dad knew he would 'cause Wayne is a lefty. Daddy ducked, throwing Wayne off balance and then hammered him with a right. Wayne was down. And out. Daddy nodded to Mama, who was looking on in abject horror, and said, 'When Wayne comes to, tell him to hitch up the horses.'"

"Wow," I said. "Your dad was really scary."

"That's just how it was when I was growing up. I'd go to school and see kids with big bruises and welts all over their bodies. Teachers beat 'em, and then at home their folks would beat again for having messed up at school. I didn't think twice about it. It was normal."

By then Glen and I were walking back to his parents' lovely ranch-style house. When we arrived, Glen didn't want to go in right away. He sat on the porch and started telling me another story.

"I built this house for my parents when I hit it big. When I was growing up, we lived in a house with no insulation. It was built on cinder blocks, and I could see the ground beneath, through the floorboards. That reminds me of the time I disobeyed Daddy. I wasn't as brave as Wayne, but in my own way I rebelled. It happened because we had an early harvest of cotton. We were able to pick the bolls clean earlier than usual. That meant we were ahead of the game. I was all of thirteen then and wild for cowboy movies, especially the singing cowboys like Roy Rogers and Gene Autry. Because our work had been done, I asked Daddy if I could go to the picture show. He said yes. But come Saturday, the day he promised I wouldn't have to work, he changed his mind. 'There's more to do than I had reckoned,' he said.

"I said, 'But you promised.'

"He said, 'It's some silly shoot-'em-up. Work's more important.'

"I knew I couldn't argue with him. We were taught never to talk back, but man, that burned me up. Daddy had promised. He'd always taught us that a man keeps his promise. I decided to go anyway. I had a plan. I'd hide under our cabin and once Daddy went out to work the fields, I'd slip out and run down to the picture show. So there I was, facedown in the dirt, with old Mason jars, wood debris, spiders, ants, and fleas biting me all over. I heard the sound of Daddy's boots overhead. I kept waiting for him to leave, but he kept calling out, 'Glen! Glen! Where did Glen go?' I figured he'd get tired of yelling for me and go to the fields by himself. But before he could do that, I saw this long black snake headed right for me. I panicked. I bolted. I picked up my head, forgetting where I was, and made a crashing sound. One of my sisters cried out, 'There's a wild animal under the house!' That snake was right up on me, his beady eyes a half inch from mine. That caused me to raise up again and again, hitting my head on the floorboard. Now the whole family was crying, 'What's happening down there?' All I knew was that I had to scramble outta there. I had to get away from that black snake. I scraped and crawled and kept banging my head on the floor, my head was bleeding from all the banging, and when I finally saw daylight, I also saw Daddy peering at me.

"'Snake!' I screamed. 'There's a snake down there!'

"Daddy, who was wearing his big leather work boots, lifted one leg. I figured he was going to stomp down on the snake. Instead, the second I crawled out from under the house, he stomped down on me. On my neck. I thought he broke it, but he didn't. He bruised it real bad and then, just to make sure I wouldn't forget this lesson, he took a checkline—a leather belt with a buckle and a snap used to hook up the horses—and beat me.

"That wasn't the worst beating I'd gotten. The worst one came when, chasing my sister Jane through our house I crashed through the screen door. We couldn't afford screen wire and without screen wire we'd be eaten up by mosquitos.

"Actually, I'm forgetting about a time worse than that when me and my brother were caught smoking corn silks in the barn. 'Ain't gonna whip you for smoking,' Daddy said. 'I'm gonna whip you cause if you dropped one of those silks, this here barn would go up in flames. All our hay would burn. Without hay we'd have nothing to feed our animals, and without our animals, we'd starve to death.' After that short explanation, Daddy beat us both real bad."

The intensity of those stories and the pain that Glen obviously still suffered was palpable. "I couldn't wait to leave Delight as soon as I got old enough," he said.

He took my hand and walked me into the house. His dad, mom, and siblings all greeted us with a big hug. Then came lunchtime, a country feast of fried chicken, mashed potatoes, and green bean casserole. Glen looked at his daddy like his daddy was a king. His daddy kept saying how proud he was of Glen. Everyone started talking about the old days, just as Glen had just spoken of the old days, but in this version it was all happiness and light. They actually made it sound like it was fun being poor. Everyone had a beautiful childhood. Everyone played instruments—banjos, basses, guitars, and piano. Everyone sang old bluegrass favorites and country ditties. It was as if music numbed their pain and acted as their antidepressant or emotional medicine. Everyone was having a ball. Glen was having the biggest ball of all. They laughed at the hardships they endured and called them the good ol' days.

A half hour earlier he had described to me scenes of what sounded like horrific child abuse; now he was all smiles. *What was I missing?* I thought to myself. *Being made to drown kittens? Carrying welts and bruises and having his father nearly crush his neck—those were the good ol' days?*

As an outsider looking in, and especially as someone visiting my future in-laws, people embracing me with openhearted love, I was in no position to question, and I didn't. Learning what Glen endured growing up gave me some insight into why Glen might need something more than music to lift his spirit. Why he might need more than laughter to keep from crying. Why he might need more than a smile to hide all the pain. Alcohol and drugs had clearly not accomplished this for him, but I knew that God could. The glimpse I gained of Glen's challenging childhood helped me understand the challenges we were facing. Yet the faith and love that abounded in his family gave me the hope I needed to begin a new life with him.

That evening Glen gathered the family together, put his arm around me, and said, "I have an announcement, folks, so listen up. I asked Kim to marry me, and against her better judgment she said yes!"

Cheers! Shouts of celebration! And when Daddy Wes chimed in with, "How'd you fool her?" bursts of laughter.

"Beats me," said Glen. "But to make things even more special, Kim and I want to start our life together by being baptized. Since brother Lindell is right here—and the best preacher in the county—I can't believe that the Lord doesn't want us to head out right now and do the job while the spirit is on us."

"Closest spot is Saline Creek," said Lindell.

"Well, that's where it all almost ended when I nearly drowned as a child," said Glen.

"Perfect place for it all to begin."

When we got to the creek, Glen told his brother, "You saved me once, and now you're about to save me again."

"God's the one doing the savin'," Lindell said with a laugh.

Glen went first. Lindell kept it simple. "Do you believe that Jesus died to take your sins away and that God raised him from the dead?"

"I do."

"Then I baptize you in the name of the Father, the Son, and the Holy Spirit." Glen went under, stayed down a long while, and when he emerged shouted, "Thank you, heavenly Father!"

I was next. I was excited—excited that this day had taken a spiritual turn; excited that, in the bosom of Glen's family, I was being nurtured by people whose love of God was expressed with such great spontaneity and enthusiasm; excited that just as Glen was being born again, I, too, was a part of this miraculous resurrection mirroring the resurrection of Christ. I went under the water. The shock of the cold water coursed through my body like an electrical charge. I entered another state. When I arose from the water, I gasped for breath and heard the thunderous hallelujahs from my new family. I was freezing but ecstatic.

Glen grabbed my hand, and we made a mad dash for the truck that had been waiting by the banks of the creek, the heater running. We jumped inside and wrapped ourselves together in a warm blanket. At that moment, I knew God had begun a good work in us and that he would be faithful to complete it. Was I naive? Yes. But I now cherish that naivete. Had I been cynical, I'd never have found the faith to follow through.

On the way back to the family home, Glen told a joke I'd hear him repeat over the years. "A preacher is preaching on temperance: 'If I had all the beer in the world, I'd throw it in the river. If I had all the whiskey and wine in the world, I'd throw it in the river. So now let's praise God and sing our favorite hymn, "Shall We Gather at the River."'"

For reasons easy to understand, the joke felt a bit uncomfortable, but that feeling soon passed as we went back to the warmth of the house where everyone gathered by the fireside and sang, "Oh Happy Day"—the day that Jesus washed our sins away.

How could this new year, 1982, have begun any more beautifully? This celebration had been so glorious that I was not prepared to face the fact that, despite everything, Glen remained in bondage. His battle with drugs and alcohol had just begun.

CHAPTER 6

DENIAL AND DETERMINATION

I was going to make it right. That was my mantra. That was my mission. I would love this man with such devotion, I would care for him with such love, I would demonstrate such patience and perseverance that whatever demons assaulted his loving heart would crumble under the assault of holy protection.

No one could convince me otherwise; and, besides, I was still living the life of a storybook princess. We flew to Dallas where we stayed in the mansion of one of Glen's friends who owned an oil company.

"We're going to the Grammys next month," said Glen. "Then the American Music Awards. Girl, you better go get yourself something to wear."

So there I was at Neiman Marcus with a personal shopper bringing me Valentino and Oscar de la Renta gowns, Hermès silk scarves, Chanel shoes, Tiffany diamonds. I had never shopped couture before, and the bill stunned me. I was sure Glen would be furious, but he just smiled.

"Is this all you want?" he asked without a hint of sarcasm. He was proud that he could indulge me. And, to be honest, I was pleased to be indulged. He gave me a gentle kiss and whispered, "I'm gonna enjoy spoiling you, darlin'." I had attempted to be frugal that day. Now I was kicking myself for not getting the diamond earrings!

The Grammys! I loved being introduced not as Glen's date, but his fiancée. My bronze taffeta skirt cinched with a silver sash with gold tassels made me feel like Cinderella at the ball.

Backstage, I recognized Norm, one of my fellow dancers from *Snow White and the Seven Dwarfs*.

"You've turned into Snow White!" he said to me. He was getting ready to go onstage, so there was no time for anything but a hug. I thought for a fleeting second—would I, like Norm, rather be part of the Grammys dance company or be there as Glen's fiancée? No contest. I was where I wanted to be.

The dream got dreamier.

"How 'bout Australia?" asked Glen a few weeks later.

"How about it?"

"Ever been there?"

"You know I haven't."

"All the more reason to go."

And we went. We arrived a few days before his Australian tour and began relaxing on that country's pristine beaches. He had his wine at lunch and whiskey at dinner, but at that point it seemed controlled, so I was happy. Besides, every night in our suite he'd sing me love songs. Every night he told me stories of his past.

"First time I ever came to Australia was in the seventies," he said. "Big airline strike meant driving from place to place. Big country, long distances. By luck, I'd brought a tape of songs I'd found by this artist no one had heard of—Larry Weiss. He sang this song that was so good it drove me crazy. I played it so many times on the bus I drove everyone else crazy. First thing I did when I got back to LA was run over to the Capitol tower to tell Al Coury, my A&R man, that I had this song he had to hear.

"'No,' said Al, 'I got a song I want you to hear first.' We started arguing about who was going to get to play which song first. Being a good guy, I caved in.

"'Okay, Al, you win. Play the thing.'

"It took two notes for me to shout out, 'That's the song I wanted *you* to hear. That's "Rhinestone Cowboy."'

"Al beamed. 'That's you, Glen. That's going to be your signature song.'"

In 1982, Glen sang that song to great acclaim while touring Australia. But after a few days, things began to go south, or should I say, down under. At one venue there was an early and late show. In between, Glen and one of the musicians drank a bottle of wine. And then another. I tried intervening, but no dice. During the show that night, Glen talked more than he sang. The reviewers took him to task. I thought that might rein him in, but no such luck.

"Who cares about critics?" said Glen. "All they know how to do is criticize."

I wanted to remind him that the public didn't seem very happy to see him half-stewed onstage. I wanted to tell him that his constant jabbering had actually elicited boos from the audience. But I decided that pointing that out would only make matters worse.

It was during that same tour that a banging noise woke me in the middle of the night. I turned to Glen, but he wasn't there. Still half-asleep, I walked to the door, looked through the peephole, but saw no one in the hallway. The banging got louder. I looked around. Where was it coming from? I went to the sliding glass door that led to the balcony, pulled back the drapes, and there was Glen, butt naked and mad as a hornet because he was too drunk to figure out how to open the door to get back in. Afraid he'd fall off the balcony, I quickly got him inside. I tried to get him to go to sleep, but he kept screaming that it was all my fault; he was sure I had locked him out.

Back in the States, things deteriorated even more. His brother Shorty and his wife, Mary, traveled with us to Vegas to do a show. When we checked into our hotel room, Glen went straight for the minibar and started drinking. I was afraid he'd end up drunk and ruin another show. I felt compelled to intervene.

"Glen," I said. "I really don't think you should drink anymore till after your show."

As Mary and Shorty watched in horror, Glen walked over and emptied the can of beer onto my head. I couldn't believe he could be so disrespectful. I flipped out. At that point, I had put up with so much nonsense that I was ready to stand up for myself. I got my little one-hundred-pound body up off of the sofa, pulled back my fist, and swung my best punch at his face. It was the first time I had ever tried to strike anyone in my life! Of course, he ducked the blow and I completely missed, inspiring raucous laughter from him. His laughter only infuriated me more. I ran into the bathroom, locked the door, took off my beer-soaked clothes, got into the shower, and began to cry my eyes out. Glen kicked the door in and threw back the curtain. I was terrified! He laughed at me again, only this time he said he was laughing because he thought I looked cute. I felt stripped of all dignity and continued weeping. Apparently, that touched some sympathetic note in his heart. He closed the door, took off his clothes, and got into the shower with me. He held me close and apologized. He told me that he loved me, but he warned me that I should never tell him what he should or should not do. Make-up sex followed. Make-up sex often followed. Make-up sex has a heat all its own. Make-up sex has a way of pushing away problems that always return.

It was a crazy year. He must have done three hundred shows. Making things even crazier was the start of *The Glen Campbell Music Show* shot in Hollywood. Glen was returning to TV. That summer we lived in Malibu, my first time in such a serene setting. Malibu represented more bliss: coffee on the patio every morning as I watched the sunrise sparkle on the ocean; going to sleep each night to the sound of crashing waves; and Glen, happy at work, hosting everyone from Air Supply to Andy Williams to Sheena Easton. Television was always a great medium for Glen who, despite everything, displayed his authentic country-boy personality for a national audience who viewed him as their next-door neighbor.

One song that Glen sang during that period stays with me: "Asleep on the Wind." He had sung it in 1978 with the Boston Pops. It had been written by Jimmy Webb. Glen carried cassettes of new Jimmy compositions wherever he went and studied them like a schoolboy. Glen knew that Jimmy saw his soul with more clarity and insight than any other writer. The summer that he sang it on his TV show had special meaning to me because its lyrics spoke to what had become the fragile state of our relationship.

Love is a glass of wine
It's balanced on the side-rail of a ship
Across the sea as midnight comes,
It may not last till daylight comes
And the trip is long

And the waves are strong
But then again, it might be up there forever
I've heard of birds that never touch the land
But sleep on the wind
And if untouched by someone's careless hand
Asleep on the wind
Our love might last until the journey's end
Alive Alive

When Glen sang that song, all was right with the world. Jimmy Webb's musical creations had a way of calming and centering Glen. The song gave me hope. But hope didn't last long. His daily drinking alarmed me. Virtually every night he drank himself unconscious. One morning as he reached for a beer, I gathered up my courage to once again bring up the subject I had been frightened to mention. But I had to say something.

"Can't you at least consider the idea, Glen, that you have a drinking problem?"

He exploded. He raged. With an elbow, he shattered a pane of glass in the patio french door and blamed me for provoking him.

"Don't you ever say anything about my drinking again or mention it to another soul!"

His voice was threatening. I was afraid. And from then on, I walked on eggshells.

That same summer we spent a great deal of time with Glen's manager, Stan Schneider, and his agent, Roger Adams. After taping the shows, we'd often go out to eat with Stan, Roger, and their wives. That's when Glen started throwing back the wine and a lot of scotch. One such evening he became sexual with me, right there at the table. Stan and Roger tried to run interference, but Glen wouldn't have it.

"She's my woman," he said, "and I'll do whatever I want." When Stan and Roger protested, he turned on them and verbally humiliated them both. What had begun as a pleasant evening turned into a nightmare. Yet Stan and Roger never deserted Glen. They knew and loved the sober Glen and believed the sober Glen would eventually prevail. I wanted to believe that as well.

I stayed.

Those are perhaps the two most important words I can write. *I stayed*.

I didn't have to, but I did. I could have easily titled this book *I Stayed*, because, in the simplest terms, it expresses my ultimate choice, day after day, year after year, decade after decade.

I stayed when many women would not have. Had I left, it would have been both understandable and, at the time, even considered wise. In retrospect, though, for all the hell that was yet to come, I am not only glad I stayed, I am grateful to God for giving me the strength to stay. Staying was my moral imperative.

Don't misunderstand me. I am not arguing that any member of a relationship stay no matter what. There are circumstances— and mine could have easily been seen as one—when leaving is not only prudent but urgent. Often physical and emotional survival depends on leaving. That's true of millions of relationships. But that's not my story. My story is about staying and how staying led to my own spiritual growth. The growth was painstaking because I was dealing with a man afflicted with, at different times, two distinct diseases. In the summer of 1982, I was not aware of the first disease. I simply called it heavy drinking.

My ignorance didn't last long. I've always been a conscientious student and realized the need to study the phenomenon of out-of-control drinking. I secretly read some books, each of which argued with absolute certainty that drinking, like diabetes, is a physical illness. Naturally it has psychological ramifications, but its origins are physiological. *The Booze Battle* by Ruth Maxwell was especially enlightening. She pointed out, along with Lois Wilson, founder of Al-Anon and wife of AA cofounder Bill Wilson, that you didn't cause the disease, you can't control it, and you can't cure it. Your job is to work on your own spiritual development. The most important thing I learned, however, was to stop rescuing the alcoholic.

One night I saw that Glen stumbled into the bathroom naked. I pretended to be asleep. I did this often because I feared that if he knew I was awake he would begin to rant and keep me up all night. When he did not return, I got up to check on him only to find him passed out on the cold tile floor. When I saw him lying there, a story he told me about Willie Nelson's first wife flashed through my mind. Martha was so sick of Willie passing out drunk every night that she tied him up in the bed sheets and "beat the hell out of him with a broom handle." As tempting as that sounded at the time, I followed what I had learned in the book instead. Rather than waking Glen up and maneuvering him into the bed or putting a pillow under his head and a blanket over him, I left him lying there in all his indignity. Early the next morning he came to bed, shivering cold and hopping mad.

"Why the hell did you leave me on the floor naked?" he shouted.

"I was sleeping. Why were you naked, and how did you end up on the floor?" I asked.

He paused, thought for a moment, and then an expression of concern and complete puzzlement came over his face.

"I don't remember," he admitted.

I determined from that day forward, no more rescuing.

CHAPTER 7

THE SHENANDOAH VALLEY

L azy walks along the beach in Malibu can turn the darkest mood bright, especially when the ocean breeze is flowing and the cloudless sky a misty blue. It's beautiful to see the scampering sandpipers and the children playing in the surf. After a night of heavy drinking, these strolls were especially therapeutic for Glen. At such times, I cherished his calmness and realized that, no matter how he may have misbehaved, I was loving him more with every passing day.

These were the days when he kept talking about his past. He talked about Billie, his second wife, to whom he was married for sixteen years.

"I met her in Albuquerque in 1959 when I was still pretty much broke—broke in spirit because of my divorce from Diane who ran off with our daughter, Debby, and broke 'cause music still wasn't paying the bills. Billie started showing up at the Hitching Post where I was playing. She liked to prance in front of the bandstand, and I can't lie, she caught my attention. Billie was something of a tease. During my break, we slow-danced and got closer and closer. She made her intentions plain, or at least I thought so. But when I asked her out for a regular date, she refused. *Maybe I want you, maybe I don't.* But I knew she did. And by then I was more than ready. Then she up and went back to her parents in Wyoming. Being the crazy man that I am, I went after her. One Sunday morning after getting off work at the Hitching Post at two o'clock, I jumped into my pickup and drove three hundred miles to Casper, where I spent the day with Billie before driving back to New Mexico for my Monday night show. Didn't sleep for thirty-six hours. Didn't matter. This was the gal for me, and I knew I was the guy for her. Well, I talked her into it. A few weeks after we met, I left the Hitching Post for the weekend, and we got hitched in Vegas. Neither of us had been there before. The neon rainbows made us dizzy. We stayed at the Desert Inn and skipped out on the bill. Years later, I went back and paid. Back then, we were stone broke. We snuck in to see Bobby Darin when "Splish Splash" and "Mack the Knife" were his two smash hits. I was green with envy. His show was so classy. He had his own big band. I listened to his guitarist, thinking I could outplay the dude. When Billie and I got back to Albuquerque, I got with my friend Norman, the steel guitarist who'd turned me on to Django Reinhardt. That made me practice ten times more than I usually did. Django inspired me to up my game. I told Billie that New Mexico wasn't doing it for me. I wanted California. I wanted to make it in LA. It was 1960, and LA was the recording capital of the world. I knew there were some slick gunslinging guitarists out there, but I was feeling cocky enough to think I could outgun any of them. Being a small-town girl, Billie wasn't sure about the move. I knew she could find work there as a hairstylist until I started making money with my music.

"'You go first,' she said. 'See what it's like.'

"I did and liked it just fine. Less than a month later, Billie and I made the drive in her '57 Chevy across New Mexico, through Arizona, into California. We had $300 between us. We checked into a dumpy motel before finding a dumpy house for $105 a month. Found me a job down in Anaheim near Disneyland, but on payday the club owner disappeared. Billie and I lived on fifteen-cent tacos. She got a job as a cashier. I hustled my head off. Found work singing background on Ricky Nelson songs, and he asked me to go on tour with him playing guitar. What little money I made, I sent back to Albuquerque for my daughter, Debby. Had my first experience with screaming fans when I played rock and roll with Jimmy Seals and Dash Crofts in a band called the Champs.

"On October 8, 1961, our daughter Kelli Glen was born six weeks early with a lung disease. I worried myself sick, remembering how Glen Jr. had died after only two days of life. I prayed. I've never forgotten how to pray. I've prayed disoriented, drunk, and dismayed, but I've prayed all the same. I believe in prayer. I don't need to understand why God answers some prayers and not others. I pray all the same. Hours after our child's birth, the doc said she would live. Glory! Thank you, Jesus. Man, I was elated but also worried. Still had those no-money blues. But I also had my guitar and this talent for writing songs. Got a staff job turning out tunes and, like you already know, Kim, that first one, 'Turn Around, Look at Me,' made a little noise and brought in some cash.

"Producer Jimmy Bowen told singer Buddy Greco, who sang in the Sinatra style, that I was the best backup vocalist in LA who could even harmonize with the sound of a backfiring truck. Bowen was my buddy and got me all kinds of work. I did commercials selling Lady Clairol bleach and Hoffman's candy. Then came all that session work. I was in demand. When I played on Sinatra's 'Strangers in the Night,' Sinatra told Bowen he thought I was gay. That's cause I couldn't take my eyes off him. Couldn't believe I was playing behind maybe the greatest singer in the world."

"And then you became the greatest singer," I said.

"I don't know about that. I had me some good breaks though. I met Jimmy Webb. Tommy Smothers got me on TV. And then suddenly I got on the covers of magazines. All that was great, but all that took its toll. By then Billie and I had two more babies, both boys. I bought her a six-carat diamond ring. I bought us a big ol' house. A few years earlier, we couldn't afford steak for dinner."

"Were you happy?"

"Not sure I've ever been happy, angel, or maybe I've always been happy. What I mean is, the TV show was a huge hit but also a grind. The producers didn't want me to be seen with my guitar because they thought it would make me look too 'country.' I didn't like how they wanted to pigeonhole music into genres. To me there are only two kinds of music, good and bad. But *The Glen Campbell Goodtime Hour* was number one with fifty millions viewers each week, so they pretty much had to let me do whatever I wanted. I brought artists like Willie Nelson and Mel Tillis to the mainstream.

"I soon found that being famous also meant being all over the tabloids. After I recorded a couple of hit duets with Bobbie Gentry, I went on tour with her. We were never in love, but the tabloids said we were. My wife, Billie, believed the tabloids. Every time I went to the golf course, Billie was sure I was meeting up with a mistress.

"'If that's true,' I said, 'then my mistress is Dean Martin cause he's my golf partner today.'"

"You liked being a star, though, didn't you?" I asked.

"I liked meeting stars, especially stars whose movies I'd enjoyed, like Bing Crosby, Jack Lemmon, and Bob Hope. When I wasn't touring, I was playing celebrity golf tournaments with these guys whenever I had the chance. I became an absentee husband and an absentee dad. I'd be gone for months at a time. I had my one-night stands, but Billie forgave me. We still wanted to make a go of it.

She came with me to Palm Springs for a tennis tournament. That's the first time I tried coke. I think Billie got more of a buzz out of it than me, but I felt it separating me from my soul. Willie Nelson told me that pot was the only thing worth smoking. He said pot saved his life because it made him mellow while whiskey made him mean. He spent a lifetime working to legalize pot. He had a strict anti-coke code for his band: 'If you're wired, you're fired.' Willie was right about coke and was right to give up booze, but all pot did was put me to sleep."

As we walked along the water's edge, the day had turned cloudy and a little cool. I wanted to stop Glen to say, "You're talking against coke, but I know you still sneak off and snort it." But I didn't. I just kept listening.

"In the beginning, Billie would go on the road with me every once in a while. When she stopped, I knew something was wrong, but I was going so fast I didn't bother to find out exactly what was going on. When she wanted to build a mansion for our family, I said fine. I figured that would keep her busy. Keep her happy. This was happening around the same time I cut 'Rhinestone Cowboy.' Billie hated it and belittled me for recording 'that stupid cowboy song.' I never did understand her negative attitude about the song, but it was one of the straws that broke up our marriage. Meanwhile, the money kept pouring in. Things couldn't have been better and couldn't have been worse, 'cause in 1975—sometime in September—Billie filed for divorce and custody of our daughter and two sons. She filed five days after our sixteenth wedding anniversary. Happy anniversary. I didn't fight the divorce or the custody claim. Billie got her mansion on the hill. I would have paid anything to get out of the marriage. By then our relationship was really toxic. She badmouthed me to the kids, and, I'm ashamed to say, I badmouthed her as well. We both did damage to our children. Then she shipped the kids off to school in Switzerland."

"You've been through a lot, Glen. I'm so sorry you had to go through that."

"That all leads up to me telling you about my third wife, Sarah. I have a three-year-old son with her, Dillon. He's coming to visit soon, and you shouldn't be in the dark."

"I know Sarah was married to Mac Davis before she married you."

"Did I tell you that I lived with her while she was still married to Mac?"

"No."

"Well, I'm not proud of that. I never thought I'd ever live with a woman who wasn't my wife."

"I hope you're not forgetting that you're living with me."

"Everything is different with you, Kim. Our commitment is not just with each other, but with God. We were baptized together. Our souls are already one. When we get married, it will be a holy matrimony. With Sarah, it was the opposite. I'd been friends with Mac for years. We were buddies, good buddies, golfing buddies, music buddies. Mac's a great writer and a good guy. He and Sarah and I hung out when he played Vegas. I loved his show. After, he took me aside and said that he and Sarah were having problems. I told him that Billie and I were having problems of our own. Talk about the blind leading the blind. I was already separated from Billie and lost in a fog. The next day Sarah came to my hotel suite, just to talk, saying the same thing Mac had told me: their marriage was on the rocks. I can't lie. She was hurting, I was hurting. She was looking for comfort. Our attraction was mighty strong.

"Back in LA I was living in a hotel while Billie was up in the mansion. I had a lot of time on my hands. Idle hands are the devil's hands. An idle mind is the devil's mind. To keep things from getting crazy, I decided to call Mac. During the tough time he was having with Sarah, I decided to be there for him. I decided to do the right thing. But when I called, Sarah answered. Mac had gone to Nashville for the Country Music Awards. That's when Sarah said she and Mac had split up. I asked her if she wanted to talk about it. She did. I asked her if she wanted to get together. She did. That night I was having dinner with Jimmy Bowen and his wife. When I walked up with Sarah as my date, Jimmy 'bout passed out. A few days later my divorce from Billie was official. That's when Sarah moved in with me. Mac was beside himself. He was right to be.

"I don't mind taking the blame, Kim. In those days I'd really lost it. I lost it to cocaine. Sarah loved the stuff as much as me. I was high all the time. The more I had, the more I wanted. I got so thin friends thought I was dying. I got so crazy I did things I don't remember. We were out of control, and we were also dead set on getting married as soon as her divorce was final. Our wedding took place at Bill Harrah's home in Lake Tahoe."

I couldn't help but remember that Lake Tahoe was where Glen

and I first made love. But I stayed silent. This was Glen's story, not mine.

"It was mostly Sarah's family and friends at the wedding 'cause my pals weren't all that happy with me. I do remember Roger Miller was there. You know Roger, he always has the best wisecracks. Before the ceremony, he and I were outside looking over the lake and the beautiful landscape when he said, 'Bill Harrah sure has a good exterior decorator.'"

I was thankful for the comic relief. I wanted to know Glen's past, but the stories of drugs, infidelity, and failed marriages terrified me and made me worry about our future.

"Sarah and I got a small estate in Beverly Hills where Kenny Rogers would come over and play tennis on our court," Glen continued. "I'd known Kenny since I played guitar on his hit song with the First Edition, 'Just Dropped In (To See What Condition My Condition Was In).' My condition with Sarah was never ideal. The world was saying I'd stolen Mac Davis's wife, but the world was wrong. Their thing was basically over when we met. But being scorned by the world is something that'll get to you. Guilt will get to you. We covered up our guilt by moving to a bigger place in Holmby Hills not far from the Playboy Mansion. We fought like cats and dogs. I swore to Sarah that, even though I hadn't been faithful to Billie, this time I wouldn't cheat. She'd told me before that she never had cheated on Mac, but now she admitted that she had. I wanted to know whether that affair was over. She swore it was, but I had my doubts. Remember, we were flying high on coke. Coke will kill your trust. Coke will kill your common sense. Coke will get you thinking crazy thoughts.

"The craziness calmed down when Sarah got pregnant. I was excited about having another baby. I tried to quit coke but couldn't.

We swore to help each other quit but wound up hiding the stuff from each other. Sarah's mom didn't help. She was always interfering. She didn't like me at all. To get in her good graces, I bought her a Cadillac and let her live with us. Bad move. She was always threatening to move out and take Sarah with her. Three weeks after our son Dillon was born, that's just what happened. Sarah and her mom moved out, taking the baby with them and moving into the Beverly Hills Hotel. The divorce papers came a week later. It cost me a fortune. More importantly, it cost me my son. I'd lost another woman and another child. I was low as the sky is high. Then, just when I thought I couldn't get any lower, came the phone call that almost took me to my grave. It was Tanya Tucker.

"'Glen, I heard you got divorced,' she told me. 'I know about now you could use a friend, and I want to help you.'"

"Wow," was all I could say. Glen and I had been walking on the beach for over an hour. I struggled to absorb everything I'd just heard. It wasn't easy.

"Tomorrow Sarah's bringing Dillon up here to Malibu to drop him off for a visit," Glen said.

"That's wonderful."

"Well, it comes with conditions. She doesn't trust me. She made me agree to have Steve Turner, his wife, Laura, and their two young kids here during the visit."

Steve was Glen's drummer. The implication was that Glen and I required supervision to care for his child. I felt a little insulted at first, but, considering the story Glen had just told me, I understood Sarah's attitude. She and Glen had led a wild life. Sarah didn't know me. It wouldn't take much for her to assume that Glen and I were living a wild life as well. As a good mother, she was exercising appropriate caution.

We stopped our walk to watch the sun melt into the ocean and the world turn burnished gold. That night we had a quiet dinner. Glen drank a little less than usual. The next day turned out fine. Dillon was a gorgeous child who played beautifully with Steve and Laura's kids. I was grateful to have Laura present as an experienced mom who could show me the ropes. I loved seeing Glen in his role as a dad. He was tender and affectionate. He knew these visits would be few and far between. That knowledge hurt me deeply.

When Sarah came to pick up Dillon, the departure was painful for everyone. That evening at bedtime Glen, still desolate, asked me to stop taking birth control pills. He said he wanted to have children. I had planned to wait until after our marriage.

"I love you too much to wait," he said. "Besides, I'm as fertile as the Shenandoah Valley."

I laughed. I hugged him. I loved this man too much to say no.

CHAPTER 8

MATTHEW 6:6

W hen thou prayest, enter into thy closet, and when thou hast shut the door, pray to thy Father which is in secret; and thy Father which seeth in secret shall reward thee openly" (Matthew 6:6 KJV).

"Get in the closet!" Glen was screaming at me. "Get in there right now!"

He'd just gotten back from the studio. I knew he was high on coke. Family and friends were used to these cocaine-fueled religious rants. His drug highs inspired him to indulge in a perverse sense of self-righteous piety. He couldn't stop quoting the Bible. I found that both intriguing and infuriating. Intriguing because Glen actually knew and loved the Bible. But infuriating because he was infusing the Holy Spirit with impure spirits. The mixture was maddening. Yes, it was wonderful that Glen wanted to connect with God, but at the same time these episodes, which could go on for hours, were heartbreakingly perverse. I was no Bible scholar, but I knew the difference between a literal and literate reading of God's Word. In Glen's chemically confused state, he was misunderstanding Jesus' words by taking them hyper-literally.

The Old English of the King James Version that Glen grew up on confused many country folks before it was updated to the

"New" King James Version. Once Glen's brother asked me if "Forgive us our trespasses as we forgive those who trespass against us" had something to do with walking on someone else's property.

On the closet wording, when I tried to explain that Jesus was simply warning us not to use public prayer for a show of piety but rather to pray privately, Glen wouldn't have it.

"A closet is a closet," he said. "Now get in there."

There was no reasoning with the sky-high Glen. I complied. Praying in the closet was a whole lot safer than staying in the room while Glen was talking out of his head.

Ironically, it was prayer that sustained me during these dark times. I prayed my way through many fear-filled nights, wondering what I had gotten myself into, wondering if I should get myself out, wondering if I had the wherewithal to survive Glen's coke-fueled binges.

The Bible battles went on for months. They were significant because Glen was using the Bible for one reason—to condemn—and I was using it for another—to love. He twisted its passages one way, while I searched its pages for promises of hope that would carry me through another day.

It got harrowing. One night, in a crazed tirade of accusation, he began recounting how his exes had all lied to him and ranting, "Satan is the father of lies!" He handed me the Bible and pointed to John 8:44, exclaiming, "You better not ever lie to me." When he wasn't looking, I took the Bible and ran to find a place to hide. I slipped under our massive dining table and pulled all the chairs in tight around me.

He began searching the house and calling my name, while I silently cried and cowered under the table. All I had was my Bible for comfort. I opened it and clutched its pages to my heart.

I needed God to hug me, to help me. I knew I could not stay there indefinitely, but I needed a moment to pray and pull myself together. After a while, he calmed down. Eventually I came out and led him to the bedroom, where he collapsed.

Fear at night led to frustration in the morning. That's because Glen never remembered what he had put me through. He'd wake me up with a good morning kiss and return to being the loving man with whom I had fallen in love. Sober Glen was perfectly able to discuss the Scriptures rationally, intellectually, and with love. He was a completely different person. When a few days passed without a single drink, I convinced myself he had turned over a new leaf and that my prayer—that God would show him the beauty of sobriety—had been answered.

I began waiting on him hand and foot, feeling I had the power to keep him in a good mood. I know that feeling was foolish, but, still in my early twenties, I harbored many foolish feelings. Glen forbade me to mention his drinking to anyone. So these were feelings I was forced to keep inside. And although I did make a conscious decision to tolerate Glen's emotional terrorism, I was firm in not tolerating physical abuse. That's where I drew the line and boldly stood my ground.

"The first time you hit me, Glen," I made clear, "will be the last time. I'll leave you and never come back."

He heard me.

I loved him dearly; I wanted to be his wife; I wanted children; I wanted a family. But I also wanted to flee. I found myself physically trembling all the time. Yet something deep inside said that God had brought us together for a reason. Something said that, in spite of everything, I was where I needed to be.

We were both elated when I became pregnant in July 1982.

With a baby on the way, I hoped that Glen would be able to relegate his pain to the past and focus on the future. I know he wanted to, but his addictions continued to control him. His dualistic dynamic remained the same: sane Glen one day, insane Glen another. Many nights after a show, we'd return to our hotel room hand in hand and make love, only to have Glen leave the room, claiming he needed to talk to the band about the show. He'd come back hours later, barely able to walk. I'd help him find the bathroom, undress him, and put him to bed. Other times he returned to the room and forced me to listen to him pontificate for hours. On those nights I knew that coke was talking, and, believe me, though it's nonsense, coke has a lot to say.

Our wedding date was finally set: October 25, 1982. I was fortunate to find the right church and a righteous preacher. North Phoenix Baptist seated fifty-five hundred worshippers. There were no less than three Sunday services. Dr. Richard Jackson was our pastor. Both Glen and I loved his teachings. It also helped that the Phoenix Baptists did not drink and that the deacons and Dr. Jackson played golf.

Pastor Jackson became our spiritual mentor. Before agreeing to marry us, he came to our home and counselled us about the moral responsibilities that the union demanded.

I had no idea how to organize the grand occasion and used the church's professional wedding planner. We decided to have the ceremony in the chapel and host a big reception in our home with food provided by the church's caterer. I chose a dress in the style of Princess Diana. I cringe when I look at the pictures—those big puffy sleeves and Cinderella skirt. But that was the eighties and everyone, including me, adored Princess Diana.

It was all smooth sailing until one afternoon Glen discovered there'd be no liquor at the reception.

"That's been your plan all along, hasn't it?" he asked.

"I never planned a wedding before. I didn't think about it." I tried to deflect, but it didn't work.

Glen was furious. He got into the Mercedes-Benz 450SL he had bought me and roared off. Gone all afternoon and gone all night. I was beside myself. I was twenty-three, three months pregnant, and in less than a week had three hundred guests coming in for a wedding that now might not even happen. Or if it did happen, would Glen be able to get to the church on time? Would I be left at the altar?

In the morning, I learned that Glen had spent the night at his buddy's ranch in Verde Valley, ninety minutes north of Phoenix. Apparently, Glen was fine. But this particular buddy happened to own a restaurant and, sensing Glen's distress, said he'd provide a bar for the reception. His gift to us.

Glen returned home that same day, all smiles and hugs as though nothing had happened. I had no choice but to cave. A bar would be set up. That actually saved the day. God works in mysterious ways.

My prayer was that an official marriage in a church with a pastor whom Glen respected would make our relationship right with God and strengthen us as a couple.

The wedding was beautiful. Pastor Jackson made it clear that we were entering into a sacred covenant. As we looked into each other's eyes and recited the solemn vows, "For better or worse, in sickness and in health, till death do us part," my hope was that the "worse" was behind us and I could now finally look forward to the best. I had no notion of the ultimate implications of "sickness and health."

Glen teared up when he said, "I do." I saw my dad tearing up as well, and, given what had happened the week before, I wondered if I should be crying too. When the pastor said, "You may kiss the bride," Glen lifted my veil and put his lips to mine. In that moment, I felt the world's weight lift off my shoulders. When I heard, "Ladies and gentlemen, may I present Mr. and Mrs. Glen Campbell," I believed that we were stepping into a better position to receive God's blessing and favor.

We left the chapel in a Rolls-Royce limo and arrived at our home reception. Time for our first dance as a married couple.

"Can you follow?" asked Glen.

"Yes, I can, sweetheart," I said, "but the real question is, can you lead?"

He led flawlessly as Waylon Jennings serenaded us with "Amanda"—not the record, but Waylon himself.

Glen took my mom aside and congratulated her on the occasion of her soon becoming a grandmother. I hadn't yet told her. Not exactly the best way of breaking the news, but what could I do? The champagne was flowing, and Glen was flowing with it. Fortunately, his mood never lost its golden glow.

During our glorious honeymoon at the Grand Canyon, I rediscovered the joy that had initially drawn me to this mischievous, unpretentious Arkansas farm boy. We now belonged to one another in the covenantal bonds of a marriage dedicated to God.

When we returned home to Phoenix, my spirit refreshed and my hope renewed, I was certain that the worst was behind me.

I was wrong.

CHAPTER 9

SHORTY AND MARY

T hank God for Glen's family. I was sure that they'd shore him up—and for a while they did. It was a blessing when his brother Shorty and Shorty's wife, Mary, offered to move in with us. Their only motivation was to help me keep Glen on the straight and narrow.

Shorty was sunshine, always cheerful and brimming with energy. He awoke with the sun and picked oranges from the trees to squeeze fresh juice. A thin, blonde woman in her fifties with deep smoker's wrinkles around her mouth, Mary began each day feeding the hummingbirds and watching the baby quail running after their mama into the cactus bed. She was a wellspring of country wit and wisdom.

Their presence made Glen happy. He and Shorty were both masters of bird calls and would never tire of showing off their skills. Glen also had the most authentic Donald Duck voice of anyone besides Clarence Charles Nash, the man who invented the quacking accent. Shorty had unique percussive talent; he kept time by clicking his fingernails together, sounding like a trap set. What's more, he was an expert whistler, singer, and guitarist. That meant Glen always had someone eager to make music. Many evenings were spent with the two of them revisiting the Bob Wills Western swing songs of days gone by. I loved hearing them harmonize on Shorty's favorite, Kris Kristofferson's "For the Good Times."

For the next five years, Shorty and Mary shared our Phoenix home. They made me feel safe and warm. Without their support, I'm not sure I would have made it.

Glen's sister Billie moved to Phoenix. Everyone called her Ozelle. The oldest Campbell girl, she was twelve years Glen's senior. When we met, she was fifty-seven. Ozelle was a character, a hard-living lady with leather-tough skin, jet-black long hair parted down the middle, and big blue eyes sparkling above high cheekbones she inherited from the Cherokee DNA in the Campbell family gene pool. Her boyfriend, Tracy, who ran a body shop on the other side of town, might have been half her age. We loved Tracy. We loved Ozelle as well. Unfortunately, Ozelle, like Glen, was an alcoholic. (It ran in the family. Uncle Boo and Glen's brother Ronald also suffered from alcoholism.) Tracy's role mirrored mine. Keeping Ozelle on the wagon was a full-time job.

When Ozelle wasn't drinking, she was the best—loving, supportive, sweet as pie. But on those nights when she and Glen hit the hooch, watch out! The worst of such nights happened in Reno. It was Christmastime. Glen was playing Harrah's and put everyone up in a lake house. After one show, he and Ozelle got smashed. Then they got nasty. When I stepped in to take Glen upstairs, Ozelle got after me. "I'll kick your ass, Kim," were her exact words. I was five months pregnant. Shorty saved the day. He kept Ozelle away from me while I put my husband to bed.

That was a bad night. But there were many good nights. Big family dinners, card games, horseshoes on the lawn. and endless singalongs. The more Campbells around, the happier Glen became. He was also generous to a fault.

An older man who worked on our property needed a dental workover. Glen paid the $10,000 bill. If someone told Glen that he liked his shirt, he literally took it off his back and gave it to them. When his banjoist, Carl Jackson, said he liked Glen's T-Bird, Glen said, "It's yours."

Glen and I once had lunch at a restaurant where he laid out a fifty-dollar tip for a twenty-dollar meal.

"Isn't that a little extravagant?" I asked.

Glen raised his eyebrows, reached in his pocket, and put a hundred-dollar bill on top of the fifty. Glen didn't like to be questioned.

But Glen did like to laugh. He was really a gifted comic who could get a crowd roaring at the drop of a hat. His repertoire of jokes was vast. But as funny as he was, he was the first to say that Roger Miller, King of the Road, was even funnier. Roger was one of Glen's closest friends and an ongoing positive spirit in our lives. Great singer, great songwriter, and an even greater wit. Glen, who was proud of his humorous inventions, also deferred to Roger when it came to funny bits. When it came to kidding me about my cooking, for example, Glen stole Roger's lines:

"My wife is such a bad cook, a swarm of flies got together and fixed the screen door. Pygmies fly in from the Amazon to dip their arrows in her gravy. She uses the smoke detector as a timer. Her cooking is so bad she broke our dog from begging."

Because he wasn't serious, I took no offense. Any time Glen was playing his guitar, singing his songs, or telling jokes, I was a happy woman. Golf should have been a happy experience and often was—except when Glen conflated the sport he loved so passionately with the activity that damaged him so severely.

In January 1983, Glen took me to the Bob Hope Desert Classic, a four-day tournament of PGA pros from all over the world. It was the Palm Springs social event of the year. Who doesn't want their picture taken with Frank Sinatra, Lucille Ball, Fred Astaire, Jack Lemmon, and Bob Hope himself? I sure did. I loved everything except the drinking. We stayed in a beautiful golf course home with several professional golfers and their wives. The PGA Tour, from my perspective, was more of a party tour than a golf tour.

For three days Glen had been drinking around the clock. On the fourth day I awoke at 8 a.m.

Glen was still passed out cold. I put on my pink robe, tied my belt above my belly—six-months large with child—and made my way to the kitchen to find something to eat. I wove a careful path through an obstacle course of empty booze bottles, wine bottles, dirty dishes, and empty pizza boxes. Despite the carnage in the kitchen, the morning felt quiet and calm in contrast to the wild night that had preceded it.

It wasn't long until Glen walked in with a large bottle of vodka searching for something to mix with it. He looked awful. I could not believe that after being smashed the night before, he'd want another drink first thing in the morning.

I found the nerve that had failed me so often before.

"Glen," I said firmly, "anyone in their right mind can see that you're drinking too much!"

He raised his eyebrows as if to say, "Oh really?" Then he proceeded to put the bottle up to his lips, turn it upside down, and begin chugging it.

That infuriated me! I reached up, grabbed the bottle out of his hand, and threw it down on the kitchen floor, smashing it to pieces. My show of defiance only amused him. He laughed dismissively and then snarled at me, "Clean it up." I knew I had gone too far. Breaking things is never the answer. I sobbed as

I swept up the glass. Other people began to tiptoe through the kitchen, trying to ignore the domestic squabble that had covered the kitchen floor with glistening shards of glass.

Later that day Glen came in from playing golf, had a few more drinks, and passed out on the bed. I stretched out next to him to nap and pass the time while waiting for him to sober up. Suddenly I heard a heavy thud. He had rolled out of bed and hit the floor. I looked over the edge of the bed and watched as he wet himself. To my amazement, neither the fall nor his wet clothes had woken him from his stupor. I had had about enough of this madness by then. I took my camera and snapped a few pictures. I wanted to show Glen the images. Without absolute proof, he'd never believe me. Denial seemed to be the biggest obstacle we were facing, and I was determined to open his eyes and make him face the truth.

I framed the photographs to capture his body and not his face. I certainly did not want anyone to see the photos and recognize Glen Campbell in such a compromising manner or to have such photos fall into the wrong hands. When the photos came back from the developer, I showed them to Glen. To my complete dismay, he denied that was him. I said, "Well, whoever it is, he's wearing your clothes!"

Then I went even further.

CHAPTER 10

THE TAPES

Our life together was in a tailspin, spiraling toward a crash, and Glen did not seem to have a clue. I lived in fear. When Glen was in the booze mode, I wanted to hide but couldn't. Glen wouldn't let me out of his sight. I cried out to God for help, but help did not seem to be coming. It was like my prayers were bouncing off the ceiling. To add insult to injury, every time I tried to confront Glen, he'd laugh it off and accuse me of exaggerating or making it all up. To him, I was needlessly overreacting. He had no memory of his belligerence.

I confided in Carl Jackson one night after a show, telling him about Glen's drunken rages and convenient amnesia. I told him about how it frustrated me that Glen could behave so horribly while under the influence and then have no memory of his behavior the next morning. Carl suggested concealing a tape recorder and recording the next time Glen was in his Mr. Hyde mode. The opportunity came quickly.

Glen's parents had come to Phoenix to visit us. His dad suffered from asthma so he walked around complaining incessantly, "I can't breathe through my mouth or my nose either." This began to fray Glen's nerves. We took Daddy Campbell to the hospital more than once for adrenaline shots to open up his airways, but as soon as the medicine wore off, he began the routine again, walking around making weird noises and saying over and over, "I can't breathe, I can't breathe."

Although Glen loved his dad dearly, he was growing irritated. Because of that, I feared he'd start drinking. My fear proved true. During one of those nights of Glen's drunken rage, I followed through on Carl's suggestion and concealed a tape recorder in the pocket of my robe.

As the night progressed, Glen slammed doors, yelled at his father, and berated his mother until she cried and locked herself in her room. Everyone disappeared. I crawled on my hands and knees, hiding behind couches to record the episode. He continued walking around by himself, ranting and screaming at the top of his lungs, "May my mother rot in hell!"

The next day, when I knew Glen was completely sober, I walked up to the bed where he was reclining, placed the recorder beside him on the bed, and said, "I think you should listen to this." Then I walked out. I was afraid that if I stayed, he'd throw the recorder across the room without listening to the tape. I hoped that if I left, curiosity would get the best of him and he would listen to the whole thing. He actually did.

He never said anything to me about it, but it must have done something because not long after that incident, Glen announced to me that he had stopped drinking. I hugged him and thanked him. I thanked and praised God. I had waited so long to hear those words. I was so tired of living on edge and walking on eggshells. My prayers had finally been answered, and now we could live happily ever after. Or so I thought.

A few days later we boarded a plane to go on a trip. The flight attendant came to take our drink orders, and Glen ordered a glass of wine. I was crushed. Tears began rolling down my cheeks.

"Glen, you told me you stopped drinking!" I cried.

He looked at me, very matter-of-factly, and said, "I did. I quit drinking whiskey and beer." He then piously explained that even Jesus drank wine and that red wine is good for your health.

Most people who battle alcohol addiction experience false starts, relapses, and setbacks. They rationalize and bargain. Glen was no exception. But the fact that he was trying to stop meant the world to me. I was not going to give up.

One setback, though, was especially dramatic. It was the night that Mick Fleetwood invited Glen to hang out with him in a Phoenix studio. Glen never came home that night.

Next morning, he and Mick showed up in a limo. I had been sweeping up a little mess in the kitchen and still had the broom in my hand when I walked into the garage to greet them. Glen got out of the car first. His dilated pupils told the story of the chemicals still coursing through his body. When Mick got out of the car and saw my broom, he ducked as if I was going to swing it at him. He had obviously heard the legend of Willie Nelson's wife. I had no intention of confronting Glen when he was under the influence or in front of his friend. The truth is that I was a huge Fleetwood Mac fan, so I was willing to give the group's founder a pass. I just smiled and said, "Come on in and we'll fix you both something to eat."

Shorty and Mary were always ready to cook a big country breakfast of eggs, biscuits, gravy, and fresh-squeezed orange juice from our orchard. I set the table, everyone relaxed, and we had a beautiful meal. We all ignored the elephant in the room. Glen and

Mick were high as kites! I hoped that a hearty breakfast would help bring them down.

After Mick left, I looked Glen straight in the eyes. He clenched his teeth in a guilty smile, as Glen would say, "like a dog sh**t-ting peach seeds!" I knew what I had to do. I told Glen bluntly, "I know you've been doing cocaine, and I'm not going to raise a baby around drugs." He just looked at me defiantly and said, "Well, you're not taking my baby."

I replied firmly, "You can tell that to my lawyer!"

My stern resolve caught him by surprise. I don't think he ever thought I would put my foot down. He bit his lower lip and began to cry. He looked helpless as he said, "I make one mistake and you're ready to leave me!"

I was surprised by his sudden change of sentiment and moved by his vulnerability. I drew closer to him and said, "I don't *want* to leave you. It's very simple. Just don't do drugs and I'll stay." That was not the end of our struggles, but so far as I know, that was the last time Glen ever snorted cocaine.

On April 19, 1983, Glen did a private show for the Firestones of the famous tire firm at their Phoenix estate just minutes from our house. After the show, we came home to get ready for bed. Glen had been on his best behavior because I was nine months preg-nant and due any day. We were just climbing in bed for the night when suddenly my water broke. We rushed to the hospital and that night, with Glen by my side, I gave birth to our first child, Nicklaus (after Jack) Caledonia Campbell. We were ecstatic!

Glen regretted not being able to be there much for his previous children when they were growing up. He did not want to make the same mistakes with Cal. He was determined to take our baby with us everywhere. Cal was the center of our lives and, thankfully, by this time, the good days were outnumbering the bad.

Our baby boy brought joy into our home and focus into our relationship. We loved being parents and took Cal with us everywhere. During Glen's shows, an open Ovation guitar case served as Cal's stage-side bassinet. Hope had returned to my heart. I could see Glen developing into the responsible father I believed he could be.

Blessings were falling from the sky. One day an old beat-up school bus, adorned with colorful graffiti and loaded with festive hanging piñatas, pulled up to our house. I looked through the living room window and called out to Glen.

"Honey, there's someone in a school bus ringing our bell."

"I know, I know," Glen said with all the excitement of a schoolboy whose best friend had just come over to play. "Come on. We're going for a ride."

When we boarded the bus, we were graciously welcomed by a free-roaming chicken, Waylon Jennings, and Jessi Colter.

"Have a seat." Waylon grinned. "We're going for a desert drive."

It just doesn't get cooler than that, friends. Sometimes I had to pinch myself. Away we went. As we toured the cactus lands of Arizona, Waylon and Glen sang, reminisced, and discussed their musical endeavors and projects.

Waylon told Glen he was looking for a song to record in a

superstar collaboration with Willie Nelson, Johnny Cash, and Kris Kristofferson. Glen thought about it for a minute and then got so excited he almost jumped out of his skin.

"I've got the perfect song," he exclaimed. "It was the title song of an album I did with Capitol Records, but right when it was about to be released, Capitol hired a new executive who wanted me to change directions and start recording songs like 'My Sharona.'"

Waylon made a horrible face, "My Sharona?"

"I told that guy to stick it where the sun don't shine and I left Capitol," said Glen. "They released the album to fulfill their contract but never promoted it. If they had, it would have been a smash hit. It's one of the best songs Jimmy Webb has ever written."

As they say, the rest is history. Jennings, Cash, Nelson, and Kristofferson not only recorded the song "Highwayman," they made it the title song for the first release from their supergroup, eponymously named The Highwaymen. It became a number one platinum album, and the song had a twenty-week run in the number one spot on the Hot Country Songs Billboard. The song also won Jimmy Webb a Grammy for Best Country Song in 1986. And to think, it all started on a school bus field trip with a chicken.

CHAPTER 11

FROM DEFEAT TO DEFIANCE

Shorty and Mary, my main supporters, were back in Arkansas for a few days. Glen, Cal, and I were home alone. Glen had agreed to go along with my mandate: no booze in the house. Unfortunately, I'd forgotten about a series of collector decanters from the Bing Crosby National Pro-Am golf tournament. Glen hadn't. He got hold of the bottles that I'd put in the linen closet and drank himself into another crazed rage. This one was bad. This one had him pointing a pistol at me. He leveled the gun at me as if he were lining up a target. I froze. Then, without a word, he turned and walked the other way.

I was scared to death. I felt so stupid for having had a baby with an alcoholic. Now our very lives were at risk. I ran into our bedroom and bolted the door. I lifted Cal from his bassinet and ran into the bathroom and turned the lock. Glen pounded on the door, demanding that I open it. We had a phone in the bathroom, but I was afraid to call the police. Bloody, awful scenarios started running through my mind: *What if he finds a way to get in and shoots me? What if I call the cops and he shoots a police officer? What if they shoot him?* I was shaking all over and praying like I'd never prayed before. Then I heard the gun go off in the backyard. I didn't know what to do. *Did Glen just shoot himself?* I waited breathlessly, weighing my options. Open the door? Call the police? I didn't know what to do. Then I heard the gate bell go off and a car go through.

That meant he was driving drunk and perhaps with a loaded gun in the car.

I knew Glen would end up dead if I left him, but how could I stay? I began sobbing and crying out to God: "I can't do this anymore! I can't!" But even as the words were leaving my mouth, Philippians 4:13 came to my mind: *"I can do all things through Christ who strengthens me."*

This word from God filled me with strength and turned my defeat into defiance. I decided that I would no longer let Glen make the rules. Surely God didn't want me to put myself at risk or to shoulder this weight alone. He had surrounded us with people who loved us for a reason. *I can do it*, does not mean *I can do it by myself.* God created us as social beings who live in community. We rely on each other for strength, comfort, admonishment, and encouragement. I was going to break my vow of silence—my pledge to Glen that I would not discuss his drinking with anyone and reach out for help.

When Shorty and Mary returned, I told them about the incident with the gun. Shorty took the gun away and locked it up. He had a heart-to-heart talk with Glen. He said, "Brother, if you don't change your ways, you're gonna wind up like Elvis—dead before your time." I also reached out to Bud Glaze, a deacon from North Phoenix Baptist Church whom Glen respected. Bud lovingly confronted Glen about his drinking. Soon my husband realized that this insanity was obvious to everyone around him. The only person he was fooling was himself.

Possibly the man who brought home the message with the most impact was Gene Autry, Glen's childhood idol. Not only had Glen seen the singing cowboy's films in that little theater in

Delight, Arkansas, he had recorded Marty Robbins's touching tribute song, "Gene Autry, My Hero."

When Ronald Reagan was president, Glen and I attended a White House reception with Gene Autry and his wife, Jackie. That's when Gene told about the time young actor Ronnie Reagan had come to him for advice. "Get yourself a good agent," Gene told him. So as we passed through the reception line and Gene greeted the president, his first remark was, "Well, Ronnie, I see you finally got yourself a *damn* good agent!" In such an august setting, Glen was on his best behavior that night. But during another social occasion a few weeks later, with Gene and Jackie also in attendance, Glen drank to excess and acted the fool.

That prompted me to follow through on my plan to ask for help. I called Jackie to ask whether she thought Gene might talk to Glen. That's when she said Gene had fought his own battle with alcoholism and would welcome the chance to bring up the subject. The two men got together and, from what Glen said, Gene pulled no punches. He frankly said that Glen's out-of-control drinking would inevitably destroy his life.

The more people confronted Glen, the more Glen began confronting himself. There was also an additional motivation: the growth of our family. Glen was increasingly relishing the role of father. Shannon Webb Campbell was born January 15, 1985. We named him after Jimmy Webb, hoping some of the songwriter's supernatural talent might take hold on our son. It did; Shannon is a fabulous singer-songwriter. Like Cal, he also slept in the backstage bassinet guitar case. Both boys grew up on the side of the stage. By age five, Cal was playing drums on "Milk Cow Blues" with Glen at Wembley and also performed with his dad on a Smothers Brothers reunion TV show. Today, Cal plays with musician Beck Hansen.

One of the most beautiful facets of Glen's personality was his open heart. Aspiring songwriters were always handing him tapes of songs they'd written. Most entertainers pretend to be polite only to discard the tapes later. Glen actually listened to them.

"You never know what you might hear," he said. "Besides, I started out with nothing and came from nowhere. I never want to be the kind of person who acts so high and mighty he won't even listen to some stranger's music."

In this case it wasn't a stranger but a stranger's wife. She was a flight attendant who approached us as we walked through the airport in Atlanta. She spoke in a lilting Georgian accent and asked if Glen would possibly listen to her husband's music. Glen said sure and graciously accepted the cassette she handed him. He liked what he heard and gave the man a job writing for our publishing company. The man's name was Alan Jackson. The rest, as they say (and I get to say that a lot), is history.

The joyous completion of our little family arrived on December 8, 1986, when Ashley Noel entered the world. Our precious daughter's eyes sparkled with every smile. From day one, she had Daddy wrapped around her little finger. Her birth made Glen so happy that, for the first time, he decided to take a year off to stay home and spend time with us. Things felt solid and safe—so much so that Mary and Shorty decided to go back to Arkansas. They were sure I could handle it from here. They were sure the really tough times were over. If only.

CHAPTER 12

THE MEN'S GRILL

The good news is you don't have to be perfect before you give your life to God. Give your life to God and then he will begin to change and perfect you. After all, we cannot fix ourselves. Sometimes change is instantaneous, and sometimes it is incremental. Sometimes the hard part is waiting on the Lord.

My earlier prayers were all supplications. "Please cure my husband. Cure him of his disease. Please do it now. Do it today. Do it tonight. I can't take any more."

My patience was running out. One day I prayed for patience and then got stuck in traffic for two hours, so I decided it was best not to pray for patience. I still had a lot to learn about the fruit of the Spirit: "Love, joy, peace, patience, kindness, goodness, faithfulness, gentleness, and self-control" (Galatians 5:22–23 CEB). I needed to pray for those very things, and what came next would prove it.

When Ashley was still an infant, I lived through an incident that challenged me mightily. It happened after Glen had sworn off drinking. I had planned our family dinner for six o'clock. Earlier that afternoon Glen had gone to the country club to play golf. That meant he'd be home by four. By five he hadn't arrived. That's when I started worrying. Five thirty had me even more worried. I called the club. I was told he had finished his round an hour ago. A bad sign. I asked to be connected to the Men's Grill where the golfers hang out for what they called the nineteenth hole. The nineteenth hole might as well be called the drinking hole.

The receptionist said that yes, Glen was there; and yes, she'd be happy to put him on the line. I waited for a minute, then two, then three. My heart sank. Glen wasn't coming to the phone. I just knew he was drinking.

A hot wave of angry resolve washed over me. *How could he do this? I'm home with our three little children. The food is on the table. And this man is too busy throwing back booze to even come to the phone. Oh no, not this time!*

I left the boys with our housekeeper, put Ashley in the car seat, and drove to the club. Women were strictly prohibited from the Men's Grill, but I didn't care. I wasn't about to be stopped. As I marched in with Ashley in my arms, there was dead silence. The room was filled with golfers. Glen was at table with three other guys. They all had drinks. I walked up to Glen and, without saying a word, I handed Ashley to him. Then I turned on my heels and walked out. As I was leaving, I heard the sound of a room full of men simultaneously taunting, "Ooooh!"

That frightened me. I wondered if perhaps I had gone too far. Would embarrassing Glen in front of his friends only make things worse? Would public shaming only ignite his fury? I worried what might happen once we got home. I hoped that the little bundle of love that I had left with him would compel him to stay calm. But I really didn't know.

In a state of confusion, I went to the women's room, entered one of the stalls, and lost control. I broke down and wept like a child. All my actions had been instinctual. I was desperate to make Glen see the risk he was taking. By bringing Ashley and placing her in his arms, I was trying to say, "Think about what you're doing. You're a father, you're a husband. You have responsibilities. You can't drink those responsibilities away." But in doing so, had I made the biggest blunder of my life?

While I was sobbing, Glen walked into the women's room and called my name.

"I can hear you, Kim," he said. "I know you're in there. Just come on out and let's go home."

I came out. He handed me Ashley and the three of us walked to the car. It was as though my sudden appearance at the Men's Grill had both shocked and sobered him up. Either way, I wasn't about to take any chances, so I drove. I expected some kind of outburst. None came. When we arrived home, dinner was on the table. We said grace. We ate. Still no lecture. Still no explosion or reprisal.

From that point forward, Glen stopped drinking.

Writers wiser than me have said most stories naturally break down into three acts. If that's the case, I see Glen's embrace of sobriety as the happy conclusion of the first phase of our life together. The second phase, a gloriously happy one, is all about maturation. As we grew in our faith and our love for each other, we finally began to bear the fruit of the Spirit. We matured as a couple and as children of God.

It was all about family bike rides and floating on the Salt River in inner tubes. Back home, at the end of each day, Glen, like a little kid, would shout "Sunset!" and we'd pile into the car and arrive at a high vantage point of Camelback Mountain to watch the desert sand turn golden.

To beat the heat, Glen was up at the crack of dawn and out on the links wearing a terry cloth hat soaked in ice water to protect his skin from the 115-degree sun. That scorching sun is one of the reasons we took the scenic route through the red rocks of Sedona's Monument Valley and found ourselves at the gate of Forest Highlands, a community that sat at an elevation of seven thousand feet and offered a cool alternative to the dry heat of Phoenix. There were fishing ponds, playgrounds, campgrounds, and a world-class golf course. We bought an aspen-wooded lot on a ridge overlooking the tenth hole, hired an architect, and soon had ourselves a summer home that served everyone's needs. Our rustic dwelling was constructed with tall vaulted ceilings supported by large round beams made of whole stripped tree trunks. The two-story fireplace was built from stones collected from our lot. We looked out across an aspen grove to a range of snow-capped mountains. Tori, our faithful German shepherd, roamed freely. So did the kids. Glen, guitar in his arms, sang songs of faith every night. His essence had returned, his gentle heart on full display.

Sometimes when the children were in bed, we'd sit outside and marvel at the black velvet sky sparkling with a million stars. He spent many of those nights reflecting again about his childhood. It was clear that my husband had survived a long series of traumas. He nearly drowned when he was a toddler. He grew up cold and hungry. He was forced to work in the fields. His father had beaten him and his brothers. He was separated from his first five children. He was taken advantage of by incompetent executives and music business opportunists. His own blunders, weaknesses, and shortcomings were gossiped about, exaggerated, and publicly broadcast around the world. No wonder he went into denial and tried to drown his pain.

Glen told me how happy he was to finally be able to be a real dad. He shared with me that he prayed every night that God would help him be a good one. He wanted to teach our children God's ways so that they wouldn't make the same mistakes he had made.

"When I was growing up," he said. "Dad was more than hard on us. Heck, by today's standards, his style of discipline bordered on child abuse. But it wasn't. We all knew that Dad loved us, and that was the important difference. As long as we obeyed him, worked hard, and pulled our weight, he was the most fun and loving man you'd ever seen. With twelve mouths to feed, Daddy *had* to be hard. It was a matter of survival."

He was also concerned that our kids would grow up so coddled and privileged that they wouldn't develop the discipline to work hard or the instinct to survive. He worried that perhaps because he was raised so harshly, he might be too soft on his own children.

Indeed, most of the time I was the parent who played the heavy. I had to be that way with Glen, so I fell into that role naturally. Nevertheless, when he had to back me up, he did it with godly gusto. I actually think we complemented each other quite well.

Now with God in his life, he had the courage to admit his weaknesses and the strength to defeat his demons. Glen had become the father and husband he had always wanted to be. His memories now came from a different perspective that carried a sense of gratitude.

"You know I'm not a braggart, Kim," he said. "You know I'm grateful for everything I have, but you're looking at a guy who's gone from rags to riches. Now, most people wouldn't see that as a problem. Most people would call that a blessing. And it is. But it's also something that can mix you up. People look at you and treat you differently. Everyone wants a piece of you, so you just start giving your time, your money, and yourself away. Pretty soon you don't know who your real friends are and who is just using you.

"I think about Elvis a lot because I believe Elvis had this problem. Elvis was famous for giving his friends cars. I've done the same. And I've wondered, did Elvis do it because he felt guilty that he had so much money? Or did Elvis do it because he made so much money, he no longer knew the value of money? Did Elvis become a drug addict 'cause he couldn't handle going from dirt poor to superrich in a single lifetime? Did that make him crazy? Did that make me crazy?"

"It's a lot to handle," I said.

"A whole lot.

"And maybe it's one of the reasons Elvis and I liked to get high. When you're high, you don't have to look at all the dirt on the ground. You're up in the clouds. Being high feels good until you come down. If it hadn't been for you when I crashed, no telling where I'd be."

"It wasn't me who saw you through, Glen. It was God. God is faithful even when we're not."

"You're right, angel. It's time for me to give God the glory. I want to sing about him. Tell the world about him. Testify like I've never testified before."

When Glen spoke like that, my heart sang. But he did more than speak about giving glory to God on those on star-filled nights when he and I were alone. He put his words into action. We went to church. Bible study every Sunday at 9:00 a.m.; the big church, as kids called it, at 11:00 a.m.; a Sunday night service; and Wednesday night Bible class. Glen was on fire for the Lord and growing spiritually. It was beautiful to behold.

I loved listening to the discussions Glen had with his mother about God. She visited us often and, of course, we'd invite her to church. That wasn't easy, because as a lifelong member of the Church of Christ, she had little patience with any other denominations. Yet she did agree to come with us to visit North Phoenix Baptist Church.

"What did you think, Mama?" Glen asked after services.

"Well, y'all sure did talk an awful lot about Jesus," she said suspiciously.

"Of course we did, Mama."

Her feathers bristled and she responded, "Well . . . it looks like you'd worship him instead of that Baptist feller!"

"Mama, we don't follow John the Baptist. We follow Jesus."

"Well, you don't bear his name. Our church is called Church of Christ. We bear his name."

We tried to explain to her that the name *Christ* was actually the Greek word for "Messiah" or "Anointed One," not Jesus' last name. We told her the Baptists were known for baptizing new believers into Christ. But she would have none of that fancy talk. She insisted that we were all placing ourselves in eternal peril.

Glen didn't argue. What would be the point? Instead he hugged his mother and said, "We believe in Jesus, Mama. So let's just praise his name and say amen."

"Amen," Mama said, seeing that her loving son did indeed have a heart for God.

As a couple bonded in Christ, Glen and I took our Bible studies seriously. Our church taught that miraculous signs and spiritual gifts, such as talking in tongues, prophecy, and divine healing, ceased with the original twelve apostles. Charismatic and Pentecostal churches believe otherwise. They profess that speaking in unknown tongues is evidence of having been baptized in the Holy Spirit. We wanted to remain open to the possibilities as long as they were in agreement with the apostle Paul's admonishment to the Corinthians: "Therefore, brethren, desire earnestly to prophesy, and do not forbid to speak with tongues. Let all things be done decently and in order" (1 Corinthians 14:39–40).

Our studies led us to visit the charismatic Phoenix First Assembly, where we were eager to hear Tommy Barnett preach. We got there a little late and the enormous sanctuary was packed. Just when we thought no seats were available, we finally found room in the third balcony just in time for the sermon. When the pastor began to speak, a congregant close by got up and began speaking in tongues so loudly we could barely hear the sermon. Glen leaned over and whispered to me, "Now that's when it's distracting and out of order." Seeing our confusion, another congregant said, "Just want to make sure you know you're sitting in the Spanish-speaking section." He pointed to a huge sign over our heads that said ESPAÑOL.

Glen laughed. "I was starting to understand some of those words, and for a minute there I thought I was receiving the gift of interpretation!"

The more churches we visited, the more evident Glen's gift for spiritual expression. He spoke openly about alcoholism in sanctuaries of many different denominations. He also spoke about the disease in press interviews and onstage during his shows. He was eager to let the world know that he had turned his life over to God.

"I finally realized I felt a whole lot better waking up than coming to," he said. He liked describing himself as a "baby Christian" and freely admitted he had a lot to learn.

"Friends," he said, "it's been two years, three months, eight days, seventeen hours, and thirty-eight minutes since I've had any whiskey, wine, or beer."

Then he held up a glass of water and, imitating Mr. Haney from Green Acres, added, "Pat Buttram once told me, 'Glen, you can get just as drunk on water'—here he'd stop to take a sip of water—'as you can on dry land.'"

Whether he was at Caesars Palace or the Hollywood Bowl, at the end of every show Glen put his bagpipes on his shoulders, conceding, "I know I look like an octopus setting up a lawn chair." Then he would sing "Amazing Grace" and play the final chorus on the bagpipes. It was a thrilling spiritual moment.

He had no problem self-identifying as a Christian artist. When he asked Phil Driscoll, a Grammy-winning Christian artist, composer, and trumpet player, to write a sacred song for him, the result was "Jesus and Me." The second Glen heard it, he booked a studio and flew off to Nashville to record it. He had finally found the signature testimony song he had long sought:

I have sung for kings and queens
All around the world
I have romanced millions
With my guitar and a love song
From Taj Mahal to Paris
From Galveston to Hollywood

I thought I had done it all
Then I met you

Now I'm singing a new song
Making music for Jesus my king
He is my hero
He's become my everything

Now there's no other song
No higher melody
Under heaven
The greatest love story
Jesus and me

In 1994, Glen released—if you can believe it—his fifty-third album, this one entirely songs of faith, called *The Boy in Me*. That boy, who had fought a tough childhood and even tougher disease only to emerge as a blood-washed believer, had finally found his way to manhood through faith in God. That musician, who could play any genre from pop to jazz to blues to country, was now winning Dove Awards for Christian music. That man was living for Christ. His devotion was not fake celebrity piety; there was no hypocritical going through religious motions or signing off on theological dogmas. Glen lived out his faith and spiritual transformation through his deeds. He helped strangers; he helped family members; he gave extravagantly to charities and causes we both deemed worthwhile. He delighted in random acts of kindness and became a pillar of the Phoenix community, helping to raise funds to build the freeway system and support a crisis pregnancy center.

In the midst of his Christ-centric rebirth, who would have imagined that one of Glen's best friends would be Alice Cooper, the hard-core rock and roller? Alice had also faced alcoholism head-on and found salvation in Christ. Besides that, he shared my husband's fanaticism for golf. Alice's wife, Sheryl, who, like me, is a dancer, became my dear friend. The four of us often attended North Phoenix Baptist Church together.

Winters in Phoenix, summers in Sedona, the children growing healthy and strong, tour dates everywhere from Seattle to Sydney. Life was serene. As our faith deepened and our spiritual studies intensified, though, we were met with a strange challenge. Amazing as it might sound, some said we had wandered off our Christian path.

CHAPTER 13

HAS GLEN CAMPBELL CONVERTED TO JUDAISM?

In the midnineties, rumors began to fly. Even today, I'll see media reports that claim Glen and I left Christianity and converted to Judaism. Let me be clear: I love and revere Judaism and the idea of being referred to as Jewish is not in the least offensive to me. I know Glen felt the same way. When he'd read these reports, his reaction was to laugh and say, "Couldn't you say the same thing about Jesus?"

Of course, you could. Jesus was Jewish. Jesus not only knew Judaic law, but he was the manifestation of the law and the prophets. "The Word became flesh and dwelt among us" (John 1:14). He was deeply and beautifully Jewish. The beauty of Jewish heritage is what drew us to seriously study that ancient religion upon which Christianity is built.

"To become more Jewish," Glen liked to say, "is to become more Christian."

The false notion that we left Christianity came after we had been introduced to Messianic Jewish teachers who taught the Jewish roots of our faith. Discovering the Jewishness of Jesus and learning how Christianity was originally formed as a sect of Judaism called The Way (Acts 24) opened up a whole new world to us. Glen relished this new phase of our theological education.

In 1996, we traveled to Israel with our children. That's when we met Boaz Michael, a Messianic Jew who founded First Fruits of Zion, a wonderful teaching ministry. Boaz became our instructor and friend. After our encounter in the Holy Land, we invited him to Phoenix where he spoke to groups we formed to study the Bible from a Jewish perspective.

"I love this," said Glen. "Putting Christianity back into its original context makes everything easier to understand. It all fits together."

With Glen's encouragement, I began studying the Bible voraciously. I took a class in hermeneutics at Phoenix Seminary and traveled to Fuller Seminary in Pasadena, California, for courses at the Messianic Jewish Theological Institute. There was no conversion—we were proud to call ourselves first and foremost followers of Christ—but also proud to consider ourselves similar to the God-fearing Gentile Christians described in the New Testament, those first non-Jewish followers of Jesus who attended local synagogues, contributed to the Jewish community, and supported the Jewish people.

Glen and I established a teaching foundation, Torah Study Chavurah (Bible Study Fellowship), with our next-door neighbor and best friend Mel Shultz, himself a prominent Messianic Jew. TSC brought in scholars from around the world to teach the Jewish roots of Christian faith. Our study group grew to nearly two hundred people. We met on Saturday, the Sabbath, and formed a worship band—Glen on guitar, our son Cal on drums, and yours truly on flute. We produced a musical called *Purim World* that included parodies I wrote of iconic rock songs to tell the story of Esther. Aerosmith's "Walk This Way," for example, became "Fast and Pray." Glen sang on some of the songs and Alice Cooper, as the villain Haman, parodied his hit "No More Mr. Nice Guy." It was an amateurish production in the extreme, which is probably why we had such fun. Search online for "Purim

World Two" on Vimeo. We also did a Passover in our backyard for three hundred people and flew in messianic recording artist Paul Wilbur to perform.

On the secular side of life, we spent some time in Branson, Missouri, after Andy Williams built a state-of-the-art theater that put that small city on the map. At one point there were one hundred shows in fifty theaters with nearly sixty-five thousand seats, making it bigger than Broadway. With Johnny Cash, Willie Nelson, Waylon, Kris, the Osmonds, Barbara and Louise Mandrell, Ray Stevens, and many, many more performing there, we were in pretty fine company.

Branson was good and bad. Good because it came at a time when, more than ever, Glen and I wanted to be with our children. It was great having what came to be called the Glen Campbell Goodtime Theater as a venue that kept us off the road. My professional background in theater allowed me to work as one of Glen's producers. I found that especially satisfying. We put together a variety show similar to Glen's *Goodtime Hour* TV show and hired the best costume and lighting directors. I brought in a world-class choreographer. We had a comedian. Glen's show suddenly had a new luster. We bought a small house that was, of course, on a golf course. All of that was good.

But on the other hand, things were not so good—because, as the years went by, Branson came to be seen as a last-gasp stop for many artists whose popularity was fading fast. Though that was not true of Glen, some unkind critics began putting him in that category, merely because he was, for a time, part of Branson's entertainment scene. Fortunately, Glen had enough self-confidence not to let the critics bother him. He was not boastful, but he knew he was a great artist. He also knew his job was entertaining an audience, whether it was in Branson or Boston.

My memories from those magical years come in a kaleidoscope of sweet scenes and precious nostalgia. Musically, seeing Glen at the peak of his musical powers was an ongoing treat. During the course of our thirty-five-year-long love affair, I heard him sing "Wichita Lineman" and "By the Time I Get to Phoenix" thousands of times. Yet on any given night in any given city, it was like hearing those songs for the first time. The absolute purity of his voice. The wondrous mixture of both pain and promise that informed his interpretation. The sweet sincerity of his storytelling. His ability to express his complex instrumental virtuosity with effortless simplicity.

Domestically, Branson was a peaceful time. Our small house lent a coziness to daily living. Outside, we had a basketball hoop in our driveway. I can still hear the rhythmic pounding of the ball being dribbled back and forth as Cal and Shannon honed their skills and dreamed of playing in the NBA. When the wind kicked up, Ashley and I flew kites. Sometimes we faltered, but sometimes the kite soared into the sky and all was right with the world.

Back in 1990, my mother Edna had been diagnosed with cerebellar ataxia, a disease that results in the loss of voluntary motor skills and for which there's no cure. Glen loved Mom and insisted she come live with us. A few years later, my sister Pam went through a divorce and Glen generously agreed it would be best if she and her three small children—Matthew, Joshua, and Alexis—moved to Phoenix as well. Pam wound up living with us and managing

Glen (far right) with his childhood buddies Glen Gilmer and Hollis Finney.

(Author's personal collection)

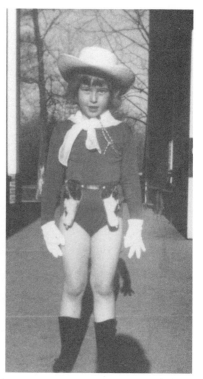

Me at age five. Marrying the Rhinestone Cowboy must have been my destiny.

(Author's personal collection)

A photo of Glen in 1958, the year I was born. L to R: Glen, Uncle Dick Bills, and country singer Carl Smith.

(Author's personal collection)

L to R: Standing: Glen's dad, John Wesley Campbell; Glen's mom, Carrie Dell Stone; Gerald, Wayne, Glen, Lindell, Ronald, Shorty. Sitting: Billie, Jane, Barbara, and Sandy.

(Author's personal collection)

Glen in his early recording days at Capitol Records.

(Credit: Universal Music Group)

Me dancing at Radio City Music Hall in 1981.

(Author's personal collection)

Waylon Jennings serenaded Glen and me with "Amanda" for our first dance as man and wife, October 25, 1982.

(Credit: Paul DeGruccio)

Hounded by paparazzi, 1981.

(© The LIFE Picture Collection via Getty Images)

Glen and I read our children Bible stories every night, standing in faith on Proverbs 22:6: "Train up a child in the way he should go, and when he is old he will not depart from it."

(Credit: Harry Benson)

Breakfast with Glen, Mick Fleetwood, and Billy Burnette after an all-night "recording" session.

(Author's personal collection)

Glen with his good friend and favorite songwriter, Jimmy Webb.

(Credit: Sandie Gillard)

In 2012, Glen and I received the Open Hearts Award. L to R: Me, Glen, James Keach, and Jane Seymour.

(© Angela Weiss/Getty Images For The Open Hearts Foundation)

Glen and Alice Cooper holding biblical harps from the House of Harrari, at our backyard Seder, 1998.

(Author's personal collection)

Glen proudly showing off his coat of many colors on our tour bus in 2012.

(Author's personal collection)

Glen receiving a Lifetime Achievement Grammy on February 11, 2012.

(© Toby Canham/Getty Images)

Glen's final curtain call at the Uptown Theatre, Napa, California, November 30, 2012. L to R: musical conductor, T. J. Kuenster; rhythm guitar, Ry Jarred; drums, Cal Campbell; guitar, Shannon Campbell; banjo and keyboard, Ashley Campbell; bass, Kiefo Nilsson; and, of course, the great Glen Campbell.

(Credit: Courtesy PCH Films)

Care team member Amanda Carungi, showing Glen who's boss.

(Author's personal collection)

Me with Glen at Abe's Garden,
a few months before he went
to be with the Lord.
(Credit: Marty Stuart)

Me at age sixty. Dancing is
still my therapy. With God's
grace, I hope I never stop.
(Credit: Ashley Hylbert)

our household. That was a way to help both my sister and our mom. Mom's decline lasted a decade. Ultimately, we had to move her to a skilled nursing home. Glen, Pam, and I were worried she'd fall into depression. But quite the opposite. She made friends with the nurses and aids. She found a rewarding social life. But then she lost the ability to speak and finally required hospice care. Pam and I were by her side when she passed. Those same nurses and aids who had grown to love our mother wept alongside us. Even as I write these words, her eternal spirit continues to comfort me.

Cultural comfort came in the form of a play that I'd heard about all my life but had never seen: Thornton Wilder's *Our Town*. Always trying to expose our children to inspiring culture, I decided we'd all watch the film version together. The kids weren't crazy about viewing an old black-and-white movie, but I insisted. We drew the curtains and snuggled up on our cozy couch. Their attention quickly waned, and at first I felt bad about forcing this film on them. I myself was a bit bored, but then the unexpected happened. The heroine, Emily, portrayed as an average woman living an average life in an average town, dies and is buried in the community cemetery. After her funeral, her spirit rises above her grave along with those spirits lying next to her. She misses her family and longs to relive just one ordinary day with them. When she discovers she has the power to do so, her fellow spirits warn her against the idea. But Emily ignores them and chooses to return to life on the morning of her twelfth birthday. As she observes her life, she's pained by the notion of how we take our time together for granted. Life goes by so quickly we notice nothing. At the film's conclusion, she asks whether human beings ever realize life while they live it—every, every minute? She is told only the saints and poets do . . . perhaps.

By the time the credits began rolling, I was weeping. Sobbing. Remembering all the precious times I had with my own mother, running home after school to hug her, looking for sand dollars with her on the beach, placing her first grandchild in her arms. My heart was breaking. But my heart was also uplifted. I resolved to cherish each moment spent with my husband and children. Yes, Scripture is a source of wisdom; and yes, I love the psalms and how they teach us to appreciate and praise God; but I also say that this play, written in 1938 by a man whose literary pedigree was strictly secular, impacted my life in a dramatically positive way.

As I faced a future both brutal and baffling, I often thought back to Thornton Wilder's Emily and her admonition to embrace the ordinary. For within the ordinary lies the extraordinary—the extraordinary joy of being here, being present, being blessed by the beauty of human consciousness.

CHAPTER 14

PANIC

Our Town celebrates routine life. Because Glen was a superstar, our life would never be routine, but, for several years, we had established a satisfying rhythm that included home, church, and the road. By 2003, though, our children were in high school and the road was something Glen was forced to do alone. I needed to stay home and manage things. That didn't make Glen happy. His wanted his family with him at all times. I was touched and even tempted, but that just wasn't possible. Our children, like all children, required supervision, not to mention the stability of a normal school regimen.

I detected Glen's growing displeasure with life on the road. After a show he called to complain about one thing or another. His complaints became sharper and his patience shorter. His demeanor was different. I didn't even want to consider the idea, but I had to. Had he started drinking? His pledge had been sacrosanct. He testified so often about the destructive nature of his disease that I couldn't imagine his going back to the bottle. At first, I put the idea out of my mind. Confronting Glen about drinking was the last thing I wanted. I feared his reaction. In the past, it triggered one explosion after another. So I left it alone.

During a break from the road, he was back in Phoenix and at the golf course when I asked him to pick up Ashley at school on his way home. When he said yes, his voice sounded slurred.

Afraid he might be tipsy, I called Ashley, who'd just gotten her license, and told her to do the driving. When a visibly shaken Ashley arrived home with her dad in tow, she took me to the kitchen and said that during the trip an empty bottle of rum rolled out from under the driver's seat. At that moment Glen joined us with a can of Coke in hand. He set it down on the table and meandered upstairs to our bedroom. I took a sip. It wasn't Coke. It was rum. Panic set in.

Panic had me ignoring my hard-earned wisdom that said never confront an intoxicated Glen. Panic had me yelling in his face.

"I can't believe you've been drinking again! Not only that, you've been drinking and driving and endangering yourself and everyone else on the road!"

"I haven't been drinking."

"Glen, I know you have. It's obvious."

"May God strike me dead if I've had anything to drink," he angrily swore to my face.

That's the power of addiction. Here's a man of genuine faith tempting God, taking an oath on his name while lying through his teeth.

"Your Coke can is full of rum," I said.

"Where is it?"

"I threw it out."

"There you go. You got no proof. If you'd kept it, you could have tested it and seen I was telling the truth."

Could Glen be right? Might I have mistaken rum for Coke? Was I going crazy? Was I falsely accusing him? That's the maddening thing about the drinking disease. Alcoholics believe their own lies so strongly that they actually make you doubt your own eyes, your own taste buds, and your own sanity. Fortunately, there was the evidence of the empty rum bottle. I told him that Ashley saw it rolling out from under the driver's seat.

"Who put it there?" asked Glen.

"You."

"I did not!" he shouted.

"Yes, you did!" I shouted even louder.

That's when he lost it. His eyes turned red and his chest puffed up. He grabbed his Ovation guitar and smashed it to pieces, no easy feat because the back of the instrument is made of carbon graphite.

More panic. I ran to Ashley's room and told her to pack her bag. We needed to make a quick escape while Glen stomped through the house, ranting obscenities and overturning chairs. We were shaking, terrified to be trapped in our home with a madman. We wanted to get out but were afraid of leaving Glen alone. We waited anxiously in Ashley's room. It took an hour for his rage to subside. When there was no more noise, I ventured into our bedroom and saw what I had fully expected: Glen passed out on our bed. I looked at him in wonder. How was this possible? Wasn't all this behind us? How could he have relapsed? How could this horror movie be replaying? Hadn't God saved him, healed him, and strengthened him so that something like this was no longer possible?

I could have been cooler. I could have prevented that confrontation. I could have been wiser. I could have realized that diseases, especially a disease like alcoholism that has both psychological and physical implications, are often not cured forever. I could have been more patient. I could have been lots of things, but I was mainly frustrated and afraid. And while it's certainly true I could have been more compassionate about the baffling nature of Glen's illness, I now needed to be more compassionate about my own reaction. Compassion is for everyone, especially for ourselves when we behave in ways that, in retrospect, are hardly ideal.

It was hardly ideal for me to continue my confrontation the next morning. But I did. Glen came to breakfast with a big smile on his face, as though nothing had happened. I handed him the Coke can I had fished out of the garbage. There was still rum inside.

"Taste it," I demanded.

He did so and said, "Baby, that ain't nothing but rum. But who put it in there?"

"You. Show me your stash now. And I mean *now*."

Sheepishly he walked to the garage and brought in a bottle he'd hidden behind some boxes. Like a little schoolboy, he apologized profusely, said it was a onetime mistake and he'd never do it again.

I wanted to believe him. I did believe him. Doubting him was too much to handle. Yes, a one-time mistake. That's all it was. Yes, my confrontation had worked because he finally admitted the truth. Yes, we could return to the wonderful life we led during Glen's long-term sobriety. This was an aberration. A simple slip. Never to happen again. I could handle it. I did handle it. Now let's just move on with our lives.

"Can you trust me now, baby?" he asked with a sweetness that only Glen could project.

"Yes."

We hugged. We moved on. Big sigh.

Big Thanksgiving holiday. November 2003. The choir from Ashley's school, Scottsdale Christian Academy, had been invited to march in the Macy's Thanksgiving Day Parade in New York City. What could be more fun? Our son Cal, then twenty, came along together with nineteen-year-old grandson by Debby, Jeremy Olson. Our son Shannon, a senior in high school, stayed in Phoenix with Glen.

I was excited to show the kids the Statue of Liberty and Times Square. Excited to be sitting in a Broadway theater watching *Thoroughly Modern Millie*, bringing back memories of my dancing days at Radio City. In the middle of the performance, my phone vibrated. I saw it was my sister Pam. I decided to call her back later. I was loving the performance too much to get up, walk to the lobby, and answer the call. Then the phone vibrated again. It was our neighbor Mel Shultz. Again, I decided to return the call after the show. Five minutes later, another vibration. Pam again, then another friend, Earl Jarred. Earl rarely called me. Something was up. I went to the lobby and called Pam.

"Don't panic," said Pam. "Glen is okay, but he's in jail."

"What!"

"He was involved in a hit-and-run and got a DUI."

"Oh no! Was anyone hurt?"

"No, he just bumped another car. Nothing serious."

I began trembling all over. I couldn't believe this was happening. My blood began to boil. Thoughts of Willie's wife and her broom flashed through my mind.

"Do not go and get him!" I insisted. "He needs to sober up there."

I called Mel and Earl and said the same thing. I knew that if they rescued him and took him home before he was sober, he would not remember how he came to be behind bars. He needed to come to the humbling realization that he was going to have to tell his family and find a lawyer. He needed to feel the embarrassment. He needed to go through the hassle of all the paperwork the next morning.

As it turned out, his pals couldn't have bailed him out even if they had wanted to. During the arrest, Glen had kicked a police officer.

Somehow, I found the composure to return to my seat and watch the rest of the show. Obviously, my head was a mess, but I remained there until the curtain fell. Afterward, I told our kids and grandson what had happened. Within twenty-four hours, the world would know what had happened because Glen's mugshot, displaying an angry scowl, was plastered all over the media.

Shannon told me the story. Glen had rear-ended someone in our neighborhood and driven off. The man followed Glen to our gates and called the cops. When the officers asked Glen if he had been driving, he said no. He turned to Shannon, standing beside him, and asked, "Have you been driving Mom's car?"

Bewildered, Shannon told the truth: "No."

Did Glen really want our son to take the blame? He was clearly drunk and not thinking straight. When the police administered a Breathalyzer test, Glen flunked. He resisted arrest, kicked one of the cops, and was charged with assault.

We couldn't rush home. Ashley had to march in the parade the next morning. We shouldn't rush home. It would be wrong to let Glen's actions deprive Ashley of this experience. Besides, I was furious. The next day was Thanksgiving. What could I be thankful for?

Thank you, God, for protecting Glen, the other driver, and Shannon.

Thank you, God, for allowing Glen to be arrested.

Thank you, God, for forcing Glen to face his problem.

Thank you, God, for the love and understanding extended to me by all our friends and especially the students and their parents at Scottsdale Christian Academy with whom we have traveled to New York.

Thank you, God, for my breath, my energy, my life, my very ability to express gratitude.

Yet, for all that genuine gratitude, when Glen called me after he was released, I was not in a grateful frame of mind. I refused to take his calls for most of the day. When I finally answered, his words were. "Kim, I've decided to forgive you."

"Really. *You* forgive *me?*"

I flipped my phone shut. Jut why did he think I needed forgiving? He was the one who broke my trust. Maybe he meant he was going to forgive me for not taking his calls. Despite his deflection of blame, I felt bad for hanging up. Just hearing his voice tugged at my heart. I was ready to talk, so I called him back. He was clearly embarrassed. He apologized and asked me to forgive him and pleaded with me to hurry home. I did.

By the time I got to Phoenix (sorry, I couldn't resist), I found him hunkered down at our estate with Shannon standing guard against the paparazzi, who'd been camped outside for days. By this time we were living in a home we had built on the Biltmore Golf Course surrounded by an iron fence with electronic gates and secluded by a six-foot-high hedge. Shannon, who had his father's sense of humor, raised life-size cardboard-cutout figures of Glen and John Wayne—movie stills from *True Grit*—over the top of the hedge as puppets to entertain the eager reporters. Drama must always be tempered with comedy. That was our way.

Glen's remorse was profound. He fully understood how he had humiliated himself and disappointed his family, friends, and fans. He didn't understand why Jay Leno had started a routine mocking Glen's arrest. As each guest sat down, Jay showed them to a bottle of Glen Campbell Hootch that sat on his desk labeled with Glen's infamous mug shot. Then Jay poured them a glass and set it on fire.

"Why's he doing that?" asked Glen. "I thought Jay was my friend."

"He is," I told him. "You can't take it personally. You are a celebrity and you messed up. Ridicule is the price you pay. It's just entertainment, and humor is a form of flattery, isn't it?"

Glen did not think it was flattering at all.

"So what do you think I should do about Leno?"

"Nothing. Jay is a comedian who's just doing his job. But as far as your public goes, your job is to apologize. Apologize and once and for all change your ways."

Glen did change his ways. He made a public apology and spent ten days in jail. After his incarceration, he did a show for the inmates. He returned to church where he was welcomed with open arms. He then did something he'd never done before. He admitted himself for a month at the Betty Ford Center.

I went with him and sat through all the family counseling and group therapy sessions. I was astounded by the similarity of those addicted to prescription drugs and those hooked on alcohol. In both cases, addiction made good folks lie to themselves and their loved ones. Denial is a problem not only for the users, but also for their enablers. I saw that I had certainly, through denial, been an enabler. I sensed Glen had been drinking before the proof was there. I wanted to deny my instincts because I didn't want to go through another painful episode. I wanted to pretend that Glen's drinking problem was a thing of the past.

In some ways, the methodology employed by Betty Ford was useful. Introspection and self-accountability are always useful. Many of the therapy sessions yielded insights. And of course, the mere fact of devoting a month to facing his disease was helpful.

At the same time, for both Glen and me, the spiritual side of the treatment fell short. I realize that the "higher power" aspect of twelve-step work has helped millions of people, and I certainly want to honor their recovery. Programs like Alcoholics Anonymous, Cocaine Anonymous, Al-Anon, and many other similar modalities have proven effective. I know that the foundation of those modalities is based to a great degree on principles set forth by Bill Wilson, who was a devout Christian. In articulating his views about recovery, he chose to re-language an essentially Christian message so non-Christians would not be put off.

In our case, though, the specific language of Christianity is vital. There is nothing wrong with the term *higher power*. I do believe there is a power higher than myself. That power comes from God, and the name of that power is the name above all names, Jesus—Yeshua—the Messiah. If someone thinks that their higher power is a light bulb, it might shine a light on some things they need to deal with, but eventually that light will burn out and leave them in the dark. The light of God will not only expose any dark issues you need to deal with, it will empower you to overcome those issues.

Okay, so if Glen was a believer, why did he relapse?

Let me tell you a story to explain. The disciples had gone ahead of Jesus in a boat during a storm. Jesus came walking on top of the water to join them. When they saw him, they cried out in fear thinking it was a ghost. Jesus told them not to be afraid. Peter said, "Lord, if it is You, command me to come to You on the water." Jesus said, "Come." Peter started walking on the water to Jesus, but when he saw the wind and the waves, he was afraid and began to sink. He cried out, "Lord, save me!" Jesus took his hand and said, "Why did you doubt?" When Jesus got into the boat, the wind ceased (Matthew 14:22–33).

The problem was that Peter took his eyes off Jesus.

Glen didn't like to be away from his family. He was experiencing anxiety and depression. He looked to booze instead of Jesus. Sometimes we don't look to God to save us until we find ourselves in a storm and about to drown. There is power in God's Word. Thankfully, Glen already had a relationship with the God of the Bible. He knew he had to ask God for the strength to overcome his disease. He knew that when God forgives your sins, God throws them into the sea of forgetfulness.

Having just written that word *forgetfulness* gives me chills. While I deeply believe what I just wrote—that our sins do drown in a sea of forgetfulness—it is precisely forgetfulness that became the focal point of a disease, having nothing to with alcoholism, that became the second great challenge of my life with Glen.

CHAPTER 15

WATER

I love the stark beauty of the desert. Arizona has a majesty all its own. But as the years went by, I realized how much I missed living by the ocean. As a child and young woman coming of age in the beach towns of North Carolina, I fell in love with the Atlantic. Loved those enchanting breezes, loved body-surfing the great waves, loved the sight of water without end.

There is an ancient Midrash (commentary) that says that after Adam was banished from Eden, he repented and sat in a river that flowed from the garden, yearning to return to his original perfection. Glen and I professed our faith in Jesus by immersing ourselves in water. We needed to return to our source of strength. We needed a time of renewal.

With all this in mind, the thought of moving from the desert to the ocean became increasingly attractive. Malibu became the ideal spot. It was only an hour from the Hollywood recording and television studios where Glen was always working. And it was also where our son Cal had moved to pursue his musical career after completing his education at the Conservatory of Recording Arts & Sciences. Shannon was still searching for his musical character—which would soon emerge—and Ashley had been accepted to Pepperdine University, located in Malibu. All signs pointed to Malibu.

Phoenix represented the past. Malibu represented the present and the future. The recent past, marred by Glen's arrest, was something we were all eager to put behind us. So we made the move. We bought a lovely Tuscan estate in a gated community and joined the Malibu Country Club where Glen played golf. I took ballet lessons three times a week. I also began classes at UCLA Extension to complete my degree in interior design. I thanked God for this wondrous life we had been given.

Before long, Shannon moved to Los Angeles, and the family was finally reunited. Glen and I took long walks to watch those soft sunsets we loved so dearly. Hand in hand, we rediscovered that blissful state of sacred marriage. We were more in love than ever.

Willie Nelson called his song "On the Road Again." For musicians, the road is endless. The road is never easy. For all its exhilaration, the road is often the most challenging part of an entertainer's career. It contains that bewildering mixture of grueling grind and electric exhilaration. The exhilaration, of course, comes in the performance. The thrill of making music. Creative energy expressed. And the excitement of that energy boomeranging back at you from an audience. You give love, you get love, and the result is a definite high. In my limited career as a dancer, I experienced that feeling. As a close-up observer of Glen's career, I witnessed the overwhelming adulation he received night after night. Understandably, he left the stage in an altered state. But then what? How do you come down? Or do you want to get even higher?

If I wasn't out on the road with him, he called me after every show.

"Why aren't you here, angel?" he asked.

"I want to be, honey, but it's difficult missing so many classes."

"Well, how about the next leg of the tour?"

"I'll be there."

"That's all I want," he said. "That's all I need."

I was motivated not only by my natural desire to spend time with Glen, but also reports from the road. Bill, his tour manager, said Glen was growing increasingly anxious and had seen him with a glass of wine on the bus more than once. My antenna went up.

Consequently, I did my best to adjust my schedule to accommodate Glen's need. Increasingly, I saw that need was for me. For three beautiful years, I made virtually every road trip with my husband. I'm glad I did. I now see his anxiety as a gift. Had he not been so needy, I might have stayed home and missed this precious period in which he remained sober.

The studio, unlike the road, was never problematic for Glen. In 2008, Capitol Records asked producer Julian Raymond to work with Glen.

"Me and Julian," Glen said after a few sessions, "are two peas in a pod. This man really gets me."

Julian was one of Glen's great champions. He talked about Glen being the first artist to have a number one song on the country, pop, and rock charts simultaneously. He saw Glen was one of the most important singers and musicians of our time and was dead set on introducing him to a new generation.

Julian had worked with everyone from Cheap Trick to Fleetwood Mac. Beyond his fine feel for Glen's talent, he also knew that the right focal point for meeting and recording Glen was Capitol Studios, situated in that iconic thirteen-story tower built to resemble a stack of records. In the heart of Hollywood, Capitol was the scene of literally hundreds of sessions where Glen had worked as a sideman. It was where he recorded with Sinatra and the Beach Boys.

Glen in his yellow golf shirt and green cap and Julian with his brown, shoulder-length hair and English bowler were instant brothers. It was Julian who helped Glen rework songs by artists like U2, Tom Petty, the Foo Fighters, and Jackson Browne. Glen met the challenge head-on and recorded the album—*Meet Glen Campbell*—in two weeks.

To hear Glen deconstruct and reconstruct "Jesus," first sung by the Velvet Underground, is transformational. He reinvents John Lennon and Yoko's "Grow Old with Me" with such sweet subtlety I couldn't help but cry for the tragedy of John's early death and the miracle of Glen's musical rebirth.

With Julian in the studio, Glen did his best work in years. His voice never sounded purer or more poignant.

"Sweetheart," he told me, "it feels like I'm discovering music all over again. I can't wait to go out and sing these songs live."

The kickoff was a release party for a packed house at the Troubadour. The critics loved it; the fans loved it even more. At age seventy-two, Glen had a hit on his hands. *Meet Glen Campbell* was a triumph, a stunningly reflective record of an artist who had reached full maturity as a loving human being.

I cannot express the longing I feel to write the words, "And we lived happily ever after." In every way, that would have made my job, and the job of our family, so simple.

But my job is to tell this story the way it happened. And what happened, slowly but surely, was nothing short of catastrophic. Yet even within catastrophe, there is hope, love, and even beauty. To find that hope, love, and beauty turned out to be the lesson of a lifetime.

CHAPTER 16

CAMPBELLOT

len was all about humor. He loved to boast how he was king of the little kingdom he called Campbellot. He said so half mockingly yet undoubtedly saw himself as an alpha male who prided himself on being a provider, protector, and lover. I enjoyed the romantic side of having a hero as a husband. Sometimes during an intimate evening, I'd hear the words of Song of Songs (1:4 NIV) singing to my heart: "Let the king bring me into his chambers."

Once we moved to Malibu, little by little I noticed that Glen was shedding his alpha role and becoming more dependent on me. When I'd ask him to get dressed because we were late for a dinner engagement, he'd say, "Okay, Mommy."

That disturbed me. I had no interest in becoming his mother and told him just that. He'd simply laugh. But the pattern was increasingly clear. I sensed a subtle submission that seemed contrary to his King of Campbellot stance. It got to a point where one afternoon, standing in our kitchen, I looked at him squarely in the eyes and said, "Look, Glen, I'm not your mommy. I'm your wife."

"But I'm your little boy," he replied.

Confused and exasperated, I pleaded, "I want you to be my man, not my little boy."

Other disturbing signs. Glen repeated himself as he had never done before. He also started forgetting lyrics to songs he'd sung thousands of times. I laughed off these lapses as senior moments.

After all, he was twenty-two years older than me. Everyone forgets. Everyone's memories show signs of wear. No big deal. I pushed my fears away. I dispelled my anxiety. No need to worry. Alarmism never helps. One day at a time. If he needed help with lyrics, that was easily arranged with teleprompters.

Increasingly, though, the repetitions and forgetfulness got worse. What I initially dismissed as normal no longer seemed normal at all. I saw it as my responsibility to take him to a doctor. Dr. Hart Cohen at Cedars-Sinai Medical Center in Los Angeles administered the Mini-Mental State Exam, an eleven-question test measuring five areas of cognitive function: orientation, memory, attention, language, and visual-spatial skills. At some point in the exam, when Glen was asked to repeat words Dr. Cohen had articulated earlier, I myself had trouble remembering them. Was something wrong with *me*? Later I learned that's common for people close to patients suffering with memory loss. The added stress of "thinking for two" makes your head fuzzy. I began to think of myself as the "worried well."

Dr. Cohen recommended an MRI and PET scan to check for signs of a neurodegenerative disease. Glen took it all calmly. In that regard, his little-boy posture holding his mommy's hand served us well. He went willingly to see neuropsychologist Dr. Minh-Thu T Le.

In March 2009, Dr. Le determined that Glen met the criteria for mild cognitive impairment. She suggested Alzheimer's could be the cause. The word alarmed me more than it alarmed Glen. She also said, though, that she couldn't rule out the effects of thyroid dysfunction or the cumulative effects of past substance abuse. Nothing was certain. At least not now.

For the next two years life was normal—attending our

messianic synagogue, doing shows, hanging out with our children. It was especially wonderful that our children had become such accomplished musicians that they would soon become an integral part of Glen's band—Shannon on guitar, Ashley on keys and banjo, and Cal on drums, all superb singers. For Glen, having his kids surround him was a dream come true. Having grown up on the side of the stage, our children were now on the stage, supporting their dad with the musical talent and love they had inherited from him.

Normal, though, was becoming less normal. Glen's first obsession involved the way cars were parked in our driveway. One evening when we had company, he redirected a dozen guests to repark their cars in a pattern no one understood but Glen. He also began suspecting a thief had been in the house stealing his socks.

"A burglar is going to steal your Rolex or your guitar," I said, "not your socks."

What I said, though, had no effect. He grew more attached to me. When I applied my makeup, he hovered over me. He was loving and sweet, but I was feeling claustrophobic. I'd politely ask him to give me a little space. He'd kiss me on the cheek and then busy himself counting my shoes, pants, shirts, and dresses. Each time he brushed his teeth, he wanted me to show him how much toothpaste to use. He would use the tiniest dollop and demonstrate how much foam it made, then hug me and tell me how much money we could save each year if we only used that much. "Campbells are Scottish," he'd say with a laugh. "You know how the copper wire was invented, don't you? Two Scotts found a penny at the same time!" This became our daily routine.

When we went out in public, Glen trailed five steps behind me. If I slowed down, he slowed down. "Walk beside me, honey,"

I urged. But he wouldn't. He shadowed me all over the house. When I asked him why, he said, "I just like being around you."

I decided to conduct an experiment. I circled our kitchen island seven times. Glen did the same. I then walked outside and circled our pool for fifteen minutes. Glen did the same. He followed me to the garage and back inside to the living room. I went into the bathroom and shut the door, only to have him pound on the door until I let him in. If I undressed to take a shower, he undressed and showered with me. (Later that turned into a blessing because he would develop an aversion for bathing.) Showering with me relieved his fear of the cold. It wasn't all bad. Some of those showers were fun.

That spring, Ashley graduated from Pepperdine and moved back home. My sister's son, Matthew Monier, had just completed his first year at Pepperdine, and we invited him to live with us while he finished school. That was a blessing because Glen increasingly required help with his daily routine.

Our routine involved Glen dropping off Matt on campus on his way to the golf course. Those drives soon became a cause for concern.

"Where are we going?" Glen asked Matt as he got behind the wheel of his Lexus.

"Just down the street to Pepperdine," said Matt.

"Oh, that's right. How's it going? Making all Q's and R's?"

"Doing my best, Uncle Glen."

"I was so bright, Matt, my daddy called me son."

The exact same exchange occurred every day without fail. Yet Matt, an understanding man, was fine with the repetition, strange as it was. But he wasn't fine when Glen's driving became erratic. It wasn't long before Glen got lost driving home from the golf course. That's when he called me for help. I drove out to find him so he could follow me home. He forgot to follow and instead zoomed ahead. The race was on. I did what I normally never did—break the speed limit to keep up with Glen. It was crazy.

When it was time to renew his license, I drove him to the DMV. He'd never be able to find it himself. To my secret relief, he failed the written exam. We went home and, after a week of studying, he failed it again. Unfortunately, he passed an oral version of the test, but I was adamant about keeping him off the road. Through sheer willpower, I prevailed.

He clung to me even more tenaciously. As I stood at the stove cooking, he kissed my neck repeatedly. It was flattering, and sometimes enjoyable, but mostly maddening. I felt suffocated and would literally have to open a window for fresh air. It didn't help that I was simultaneously dealing with the hot flashes of menopause. He was hot for one reason, and I was hot for another.

His behavior changed in other ways. He usually picked out the car he wanted me to drive, but this time I decided to lease a BMW coupe. At first, he was cool with it but then inexplicably began ranting how he hated the car. His rants went on day after day.

Our German shepherd JJ, furious defender of Campbellot for twelve years, was on his last legs. I thought having a new puppy in the house would soften the blow when JJ would eventually leave us. Glen and I scoured the internet for puppies and found a black giant schnauzer. We called her Kona, Hawaiian for "dark lady." Hawaii was our favorite place in the world, but Kona did not become Glen's favorite dog. Quite the contrary. He became jealous of the time I spent training and coddling Kona until one day he blurted out, "You love that dog more than me. I don't want you to have anything that takes your attention away from me."

I felt anger and resentment. Glen felt neglected. I still wanted to believe that nothing was seriously wrong but could hardly sustain that belief. His behavior was more erratic than ever. I felt apprehension and dread. I felt fear.

CHAPTER 17

GHOST ON THE CANVAS

God bless Julian Raymond. Musically, his understanding of Glen was eerily profound. The experience they shared of returning to the studio in 2010 to record *Ghost on the Canvas* is a testimony to the enduring power of music to heal.

Aware of the looming specter of Alzheimer's, Julian wanted to cut a record based on Glen's life and legacy. The title song, written by Paul Westerberg, set the tone. During the sessions, Glen shared his heart, wisdom, jokes, and endless anecdotes with Julian. I was privileged to witness it all. I was also taken by my husband's insights. It was almost as if his failing brain circuitry was opening new pathways of creative expression. Whether consciously or not, Glen knew something was happening to him. Julian had the good sense to take careful notes and weave Glen's thoughts into lyrics. One song they co-composed, "Strong," is a premonition of the strength and grace we would need for the storm ahead:

As I look into these eyes I've known for all these years
I see for the first time in my life, fear
This is not the road I wanted for us, but now that's it's here
I want to make one thing perfectly clear

All I want to be for you is strong
I'm going to be the one you can count on
I'll always be for you strong

I'm a broken prize all neatly wrapped but cracked inside
All the king's horses and all his men, they lied
As I look at you and at my life, what do I see?
The person that I wish that I could be

I also adore another song that Julian and Glen composed, one that transforms Glen's tender confusion into lyrical beauty: "A Better Place."

I've tried and I have failed, Lord
I've won and I have lost
I've lived and I have loved, Lord
Sometimes at such a cost
One thing I know
This world's been good to me
A better place awaits you'll see

Some days I'm so confused, Lord
My past gets in my way
I need the ones that I love, Lord
More and more each day
One thing I know
This world's been good to me
A better place awaits you'll see

"All of my little roller-coaster rides," Glen wrote in the liner notes, "the laughter, tears, successes, and failures—they're all part of who I am now . . . that's what *Ghost on the Canvas* is all about. It's the 'now' Glen with all the ghosts of the old Glens still kind of hanging around."

186

Together, Julian and Glen turned out another masterpiece. At seventy-four, Glen was still capable of incredible work. His voice had changed—it was deeper and more resonant—but he had never sounded so introspective or sincere. He mastered the new material. Julian had him playing with artists as diverse as Chris Isaak, Brian Setzer, and Dick Dale. Much like Johnny Cash's final work put together by producer Rick Rubin, Glen's collaboration with Julian represents a permanent record of his ability to grow musically in spite of—or perhaps because of—the radical changes he was experiencing in his heart and head.

In early 2011, Glen and I were driving to Dr. Cohen for another evaluation. Glen was driving me crazy, pushing every button on the dash and rolling the windows up and down. We pulled into the parking lot only to have Glen get out of the car, unzip his pants, and get ready to pee.

"No, no, no. Honey, you can't pee here. You can make it to the bathroom. Come on. I'll take you."

We crossed the street and made it to the elevator. We pushed the up button and waited.

"I have to pee now," Glen insisted.

"Okay, we just have to get to our floor. There is a bathroom there. You can make it," I assured him.

When the doors opened, we squeezed into an already packed elevator. Facing all those people made Glen forget his urgent need for a bathroom. Instead of turning around to face the doors, Glen remained facing his new audience. As the doors closed behind us, Glen addressed the crowd, "I guess you're all wondering why I asked you here today." I could tell they were all trying to remember where they might have seen that face before. "Am I who you think I am?" Glen queried with a smile. He made it to the men's room and minutes later we were with Dr. Cohen. He administered all the same tests from before. This time there was no doubt.

"Glen," he said, "you have Alzheimer's disease."

I gasped. My eyes grew wide and watery. I fought back tears. Glen wasn't fazed.

"I don't feel it," he said with a puzzled look. "I feel fine."

"That's great, but your memory will be affected more and more as time goes on."

Glen laughed and said, "Well, there's lots of things I'd like to forget."

As we left, I asked Glen if I could have a moment alone with the doctor. Glen readily agreed. As he patiently waited in the hallway, he seemed serene.

I got right to the point with Dr. Cohen.

"Is it fatal?" I asked.

"Yes."

Not the answer I expected. I felt myself going into shock.

"How fast does it progress? How long will he live?"

"It's different for everyone, Kim. Usually four to ten years from the time of diagnosis, but there are people who live twenty years. In the early stages, Glen should be able to live a very productive life."

"Can he work?" I asked. "He's just finished a record and is planning a five-week tour to promote it."

"I'd encourage him to do so. Music activates every area of the brain. That stimulation may well help him function longer. Yes, encourage him to play. And encourage him to remain engaged with family and friends. Social isolation expedites cognitive decline."

"Should he drive?"

"No. California law requires doctors to notify the DMV when a patient is diagnosed with Alzheimer's. His license will be revoked."

"Can medication help?"

"Aricept and Namenda can soften symptoms in this early stage, but as of yet there are no drugs to slow, stop, or cure Alzheimer's."

Dr. Cohen told me to bring him back in six months.

I was still in shock. Glen wasn't. We went to Jerry's Deli for lunch where I somehow kept my composure. I pretended everything was fine. Inside, though, I was afraid. I now saw everything differently. All his strange behaviors suddenly made sense. The little things that had been annoying now evoked compassion. No wonder he followed me everywhere. No wonder he was jealous of anything that competed for my attention. I was his anchor. He needed me to feel secure. Now that need was greater than ever.

That night, for all my new understanding, I was nonetheless overcome with sadness. I cried myself to sleep. I realized we were entering an entirely new and unknown chapter.

CHAPTER 18

"I NEED THE ONES
I LOVE, LORD"

I kept listening to "A Better Place" and hearing that line that seemed to address me directly. Of course, it addressed family and friends as well. I began with family.

The first people I told were our children. There were gasps and cries but, because they have inherited their father's strength, they also resolved to stay the course. Without my children, I'm not sure I would have made it through the ordeal. There were friends to tell and other family members to comfort. And then there was studying. I committed myself to learning everything I could about this crippling disease. I stayed on the internet for days, doing nothing but absorbing information. I was so grateful for in-depth websites like the Alzheimer's Association, Alz.org.

The first real shock for Glen came in the mail. The DMV had revoked his license. He read the letter and looked puzzled.

"You have Alzheimer's, Glen. Do you know what that is?"

"Well, sure I do. . . . What is it?" he said with a smile. This was Glen's sly attempt to be funny and lighten the mood. At the same time, I realized he fundamentally did not understand the gravity of his condition.

There was no way to soften the blow. "Sweetheart," I said, "it's a disease that makes you lose your memory and eventually your ability to think and reason."

His countenance dropped and his mood turned somber.

"I understand, but why did they take my license away? I'm one of the best drivers on the road."

I braced myself. I anticipated an outburst, but instead he hung his head in defeat. I let it go for the rest of the day. That evening, though, I readdressed the issue.

"You know your friend Ronald Reagan had Alzheimer's, just like you."

"I know I have Alzheimer's, angel, but I don't feel it."

"Good. That means you can live with it. Play music. Play golf. Have fun. Our life will still be beautiful. We'll be closer than ever."

Soon his golf buddies, Dante Rossi and TK Kimbrell, were reporting Glen's erratic behavior on the links. Because they loved him, they simply helped him and overlooked what others might have found annoying.

The decision to keep playing golf was an easy one. And while Dr. Cohen stressed the importance of continuing musical activities, playing and touring are two very different things. Touring is grueling, and there's a world of difference between recording in a studio and performing before thousands of fans who've paid good money with the expectation of hearing the Glen Campbell they've known and loved for so long.

Glen made the decision. He was adamant.

"Of course, I'm going to tour," he said. "*Ghost on the Canvas* is a great album and I wanna promote it. I wanna sing those songs live."

"I love your attitude, honey," I said, "and I'm willing to go along with whatever you want, but there are some things to consider. If you repeat yourself onstage or act a little strange, people might start talking. What might the press say?"

"Tell 'em the gosh-darn truth. Tell 'em I got Alzheimer's!"

There it was. Glen's fearlessly honest, matter-of-fact solution: tell the world. Why not? There was absolutely no shame in Glen's game.

Julian Raymond was thrilled with the decision. He saw it as further proof of Glen's gutsy approach to life. Beyond the tour, Julian suggested we take it a step further. Why not make a rockumentary of what would become known as the Goodbye Tour? I loved the idea.

Julian contacted James Keach, an actor, director, and producer who was responsible for, among other projects, *Walk the Line*, the biopic of our friend Johnny Cash. James and his partner Trevor Albert, producer of *Groundhog Day*, agreed to explore the notion, but after watching several films about Alzheimer's decided against signing on. They thought the film would be a downer and never attract a wide audience.

Nonetheless, James was willing to meet with us. At the time, he was married to the beautiful English actress Jane Seymour. Glen and I drove to their oceanfront estate in Malibu to meet them. I reminded Glen that Jane played the Bond girl Solitaire in *Live and Let Die*, starred with Christopher Reeve in *Somewhere in Time*, and also starred in the hit TV series, *Dr. Quinn, Medicine Woman*. James had played Jesse James in *The Long Riders*.

James and Jane were a power couple, both as performers and producers, but didn't act that way. They were gracious and loving. Jane was also a successful jewelry designer.

As the four of us began talking, their teenage son Johnny walked through the room carrying a guitar.

"Hey," said Glen. "I play guitar. Want me to show you something?"

"Sure."

Glen shredded a solo as Johnny watched in awe. Glen handed him back the guitar and said, "And that's how you do it, son."

"Talk to me about Alzheimer's," said James. "Tell me how you feel about it."

"Well, Kim knows a whole lot more about it than I do. Kim's been studying it the same way she's studied the Bible. I know it's a complicated sickness, but I also know most people don't understand it. Most people are afraid of it. Well, if I go out there and show 'em you can do a whole tour, even though you got Alzheimer's, maybe Alzheimer's will look less scary. And maybe more people will get interested in finding a cure for the thing."

"So the tour doesn't scare you?" asked Jane.

"No. I've been making music all my life. I want to continue doing what I love with the people I love. It's who I am. I want to continue being me."

We all laughed. In the middle of the discussion, Johnny walked through the room again with the same guitar in hand.

"Hey," said Glen. "I play guitar. Want me to show you something?"

"Sure."

Glen shredded yet another incredible solo before handing the guitar back.

"And that's how you do it, son," he said.

Johnny, James, and Jane were amazed at Glen's extraordinary talent even as Alzheimer's manifested itself right before our eyes. His short-term memory was clearly failing, but his musical memory was fully intact.

Glen's optimism, courage, sense of humor, and tenacity convinced James and Jane that producing a rockumentary of the tour was, after all, a great idea. Our friendship was forged, a deal was cut, and a surge of energy gave us new life. The film, *Glen Campbell: I'll Be Me*, a labor of love, would eventually be released in 2014 to great acclaim.

Back in June 2011, we broke Glen's medical news in an interview with *People* magazine and announced his upcoming tour. In a matter of days, millions of fans around the world were stunned. More and more I began to see how Alzheimer's is poorly understood. Its social stigma makes people reluctant to seek a diagnosis. On the one hand, it's often dismissed as "Old Timer's Disease," a sort of charming and laughable forgetfulness like Grandpa's senior moments. On the other hand, it's the most feared disease for people over fifty. Someone admitting to Alzheimer's runs the risk of being dismissed from work and responsibilities, intellectually disregarded, and socially ostracized. Glen's forthright declaration helped remove some of that stigma and opened up a national conversation about the disease.

On August 30, 2011, *Ghost on the Canvas* was released, Glen's sixty-first album. Critics were enthralled. They heard each song as a window into Glen's heart as his mind was beginning to falter. The fresh new sound, coupled with the emotional weight of a musical giant's grand farewell, had generated what one writer called the best album of his career.

Then it was off to the races.

We went on a PR tour, first New York and then London, to pave the way for the UK leg of the tour. Glen did best when asked about experiences from his early career that remained stored in his long-term memory. Questions requiring short-term memory left him looking to me to fill in the blanks. I was happy to do so.

In Manhattan, all the journalists wanted to know how Glen was dealing with Alzheimer's. Glen brushed sentimentality aside, saying, "I feel fine. It's just something I gotta deal with." Another interviewer asked him how he would like to be remembered. He said, "Just the way I am. I believe in God, and I believe in treating other people the same way you want to be treated, and to help others less fortunate."

In several of these interviews, he confessed to his dependence on me, saying flattering things like, "I love that verse in the Bible that says, 'If a man findeth a good wife, he findeth a good thing.' I found my good thing."

The press trip to London worried me. I was afraid the jet lag would be too taxing for Glen, so we gave ourselves a day to rest. During our first interview, Glen struggled to communicate. He looked lost. In fact, he was lost. He couldn't answer a question or stay on track. The reporter was patient and kind while I spoke for Glen. Alarmed, I wondered if we should be granting any more interviews at all. I got him a cup of coffee to see if it would perk him up before the next reporter sat down. Within minutes, Glen was able to remember things and communicate perfectly. Miraculously, he became coherent and articulate. Maybe the caffeine did the trick, or maybe this was just part of the up-and-down, in-and-out random nature of early stage Alzheimer's.

The next morning the *Sunday Telegraph* ran a full-page picture of Glen and a four-page story titled: "A Smile Can Hide All the Pain: How Alzheimer's Has Ravaged the Rhinestone Cowboy." It offered a stellar review of *Ghost on the Canvas* but portrayed Glen as pathetically confused. This was not the case.

Yes, he had moments of disorientation, but most of the time, with a little patience and cuing, he understood exactly what was going on and could function.

In a *USA Today* interview, he pointed out a bright side to Alzheimer's, repeating that line he'd told Dr. Cohen that never failed to garner laughs, probably because it's true: "There are a lot of things I don't want to remember anyway."

CHAPTER 19

A DANCE OF LOVE

E ven before tour rehearsals, we got a glimpse of the difficulty ahead. The first alarming incident came when Glen's devoted friend Dante dropped him at home after a round of golf. It was late afternoon. Dante assumed Glen wouldn't be alone because our nephew's car was in the driveway. But Matt had gone off to do errands with Ashley and the house was locked. Glen didn't have the key. He somehow managed to climb through the kitchen window that was five feet off the ground. When I arrived, I noticed the open window with the screen removed. Our dog was calm, nothing was awry, so I put two and two together and correctly guessed what had happened. I called Glen's name. No response. I called it again. Still nothing. In the past weeks he had taken to stroll down Pacific Coast Highway, and I was wondering whether he had done so again when he suddenly appeared walking toward me, wearing absolutely nothing but a big smile and his tennis shoes.

"Glen! Where are your clothes?"

He was totally unconcerned. He pulled me into a tango pose, dipped, and gave me a great big kiss.

"Let's dance the dance of love," he said.

I wasn't sure what to do. As it turned out, I had no time to think because he kissed me again, and again. I yielded. I decided that this was hardly the time to argue with him. I'd be hard-pressed to find another seventy-five-year-old man this good-looking. His body was in remarkably good shape. We danced.

Things got even more interesting when Dr. Cohen doubled the dosage of Aricept, one of the drugs designed to improve memory. As a result, Glen's libido went wild. I love love, but this was too much. The physician cut the dosage back. Things slowed down a bit, but Glen still had the physical energy of a man half his age.

I look back at these episodes with a smile. This disease has taught me to make whatever beautiful memories there are to make. Cherish every moment when body and soul are singing in harmony. Accept each invitation to dance. Love extravagantly.

Rehearsals were hardly a labor of love. They were challenging. The first job was the set list. Glen and his musical director, TJ Kuenster, front-loaded the show with Glen's iconic hits along with Glen favorites like Jimmy Webb's "The Moon's a Harsh Mistress" and Hank Williams's "Lovesick Blues." Those songs were so deeply embedded in Glen's long-term memory we assumed they'd pose no problem. The rest of the show would be filled with songs from *Ghost on the Canvas*.

With amyloid beta plaques and tangles creeping through Glen's brain, though, learning new material was an uphill battle. But Glen set out to do what every pro does when faced with new material. He studied and practiced. I set up a teleprompter at home so he could sing along to the new music. He conscientiously did so for weeks, giving us hope that he could assign the lyrics to his long-term memory. For a while, it went well.

Then it didn't. I was conscious of the need to keep everything low-key and relaxed. Soft lighting. Light refreshments. A little prayer before each session. Throughout the entire arduous but beautiful ordeal, it helped that Cal, Shannon, and Ashley were by his side. Having his children as bandmates made all the difference in the world. Yet even the presence of our progeny didn't assuage the terrible agitation that attacked Glen during those first rehearsals.

Each time a song kicked off, Glen held up his hand. Wrong tempo. Start again. Still not right. Start again. The tempo was okay, but the speaker was off. The sound was wrong. The key was wrong. The keyboard was wrong. Glen started showing the bass player how to play his instrument. Glen went around instructing everyone on this thing or that. He was clearly annoyed that, in his mind, the band was not congealing. In everyone else's mind, though, it was. But Glen's mind was the mind that mattered. He was the star, and that star had to be placated, even though the star was not well.

We forged ahead. We got through those initial rehearsals and now needed to step it up a notch. It was time for a full band rehearsal on a soundstage. We rented one in beautiful downtown Burbank and invited close friends, label execs, and the film crew shooting the doc. I was a nervous wreck. I was frightened that if Glen behaved here the way he had behaved before, this project could end before it began. When Julian Raymond, the producer who had singlehandedly given my husband a new musical life, welcomed Glen to the stage, I held my breath.

What I witnessed was the first of a series of miracles that marked this ambitious project. In between each miracle were setbacks, but I don't want those setbacks to distract from celebrating the miracles. Glen stepped in front of the audience and, after days of anguish and sometimes repellant behavior, became Glen Campbell. The star was reborn. He turned back into a seasoned performer who knew the difference between rehearsing a show and doing a show. It was the audience that made the difference.

Glen wasn't an ethereal artist who liked locking himself in a private studio looking for the lost chord. He loved people, and people loved him. He played for people. It was the humanity of his listeners that imbued his music with such warmth. He felt them; they felt him. Beyond that, he was a seasoned pro. He played to the cameras at just the right time, knowing that, like the audience, the cameras also loved him. He came alive.

Then came a phenomenon we did not expect. Seeing a group of children who had moved to the front of the stage to be close to him, he turned on his trademark Donald Duck voice. No one did a better Donald Duck than Glen. That was fine, except the transformation from country crooner to cartoon quacker stopped the rehearsal in midtrack. It was funny, even hilarious, and the kids loved it. But it wasn't exactly what we planned. Getting Glen back in focus wasn't easy. I made a silly pun, saying, "If we're going to take this show on the road, we better get our ducks in a row." That's when we decided that, despite our love for children, we'd have to make sure no kids would be seated in the first rows of any theater we played.

CHAPTER 20

ON THE LINE

Everyone from James Taylor to Ray Charles has sung "Wichita Lineman." Their versions are great. My daughter Ashley sings the song in her own wonderful way. I remind myself, though, that when Jimmy Webb wrote it in 1968, he had Glen in mind. He saw it as a story Glen could convey with that special sense of longing that lived in the center of Glen's soul. No Glen Campbell audience would allow him to leave the stage without hearing it. It became the centerpiece not only of his career but of the Goodbye Tour as well. Listening to it night after night, the beauty of the song never diminished, but its meaning expanded:

> *I am a lineman for the county*
> *And I drive the main road*
> *Searchin' in the sun for another overload*
> *I hear you singing in the wire*
> *I can hear you through the whine*
> *And the Wichita lineman*
> *Is still on the line*
>
> *I know I need a small vacation*
> *But it don't look like rain*
> *And if it snows that stretch down south*
> *Won't ever stand the strain*

And I need you more than want you
And I want you for all time
And the Wichita lineman
Is still on the line

As Glen braved his way through the ordeal of Alzheimer's, as he sang this song night after night, I heard it differently. It struck me as deeply spiritual. Glen was indeed the lineman, the working-man's singer who, no matter what, was on the road to repair whatever he could. It is surely a song about love, but I began to hear those lines—"I hear you singing in the wire, I can hear you through the whine"—as an acknowledgement of the presence of God. It was God who gave Glen his gift, God who sang in the wire of his creative mind, God whom Glen expressed as a sacred whine—a cry, a prayer—that helped keep him whole enough to stay on the line. "Wichita Lineman" became an affirmation, a musical statement of a good man's determination to carry on.

And carry on he did. He realized the significance of what he was doing. He was not only telling the world that Alzheimer's was not going to keep him from doing what he was born to do, he was also saying, "I am not afraid." When it was brought to his attention that the unpredictability of Alzheimer's might well cause him to make major mistakes onstage, his response was, "The people that mind don't matter and the people that matter don't mind."

The first show was a big one just because it *was* the first. I helped him get ready. I powdered his face and added some bronzer. I handed him his shirt, pants, belt, and jacket. I knelt down in front of him to help put his boots on.

"Hey, while you're down there—" he jested as he always did.

We both laughed. Sexual energy is life energy. I was glad to see him both energetic and sexy. I stood up and kissed him, giving his lips a hint of pink. We prayed as we did before every show. He checked himself in the mirror. The Rhinestone Cowboy was ready to roll.

His courage proved contagious. The show was sold out. Scores of fans, old and new, were eager to see him. We waited in the wings and watched Ashley play the banjo intro to "Gentle on My Mind." Then, with the confidence of a veteran superstar, he threw back his shoulders and strode onstage. The crowd jumped to their feet. It was a love fest. Glen's long-term memory nailed all the old songs. He sang the new ones with reflective grace, the old trooper still able to express the poetry that informed his timeless art.

To switch metaphors, I like quoting our documentary director James Keach, who would later muse, "Watching Glen is like watching Rocky with a guitar."

The champ wasn't about to go down.

And yet the punches came. Rehearsals for Jay Leno's *Tonight Show* were scary. Glen refused to conform to the stage markers. He wouldn't stand in the circle that gave the cameras the right angles. He kept moving around in awkward and impetuous ways. I was terrified the performance would be a disaster and, if so, a national audience would see Glen as incompetent and inept. Ticket sales for the tour would plummet. Even worse, the tour could be canceled

And then came still another miracle. When the audience filed in, when the show began, when Jay introduced Glen as the man who has won five Grammys and sold over fifty million records worldwide, Glen became Glen all over again. He stayed within the circle. He gave the cameras the angles the cameras required. As soon as he sang the opening line—that beautiful, precious, absolutely perfect line—"I've tried and I have failed, Lord"— from "A Better Place," he *was* in a better place. He captured the studio audience, captured the national audience, delivered a stellar performance, and, against all odds, the tour was not only on, but dates were added daily. Seemingly every Glen Campbell fan wanted to see him, not in spite of his struggle but because he was willing to play out his struggle in public.

His appearance on *Conan* had drama of its own. Rehearsal went really well. But while we waited backstage, Glen asked me which songs he was doing. The songs, I said, that he had just rehearsed with the band. "Who picked those songs? I'm not singing those songs!" He was bossy and belligerent. "I'll decide what to sing, and I ain't singing this stuff." He got mad and pushed Stan, his manager. At showtime, when the band was called to take their place onstage, Glen fired the band. "I'm not going out there," he insisted. "I'm doing this thing my way, not theirs." Somehow, we were able to usher Glen to the side of the stage so that he could see the audience. When he heard Conan introduce him and the crowd start to applaud, God gave us another miracle. Glen lit up and began to smile. He did go out there; he did sing his heart out; and he did perform magnificently.

"What was all that commotion before the show?" he asked me in the limo on the way home.

I played dumb and changed the subject. "You did a great job, baby. Let's stop and get some donuts."

I never eat donuts, but that night I joined Glen in a feast of Krispy Kremes.

The tour rolled on. The audiences grew in number and enthusiasm. Glen continued to have his moments offstage, but onstage he was all about music and love. We were playing Ireland when we learned that the Country Music Association wanted to pay tribute to Glen during their annual award show. So in November 2011, Glen and I left the band and crew in Killarney and flew to Nashville. We scurried over to see Manuel, the guru of country music costumery, who had dolled up everyone from Merle Haggard to Dolly Parton. Manuel fitted Glen in an embroidered jacket to coordinate with my Ralph Lauren gown. My husband looked absolutely regal. Onstage, Vince Gill sang "By the Time I Get to Phoenix," Keith Urban sang "Wichita Lineman," and Brad Paisley sang "Galveston." Sitting beside me, Glen watched from the front row and sang along *without* a teleprompter. The industry's most prominent artists praised him to the sky. Thankfully, he was present. He took it all in. I've never seen him happier.

Back in Killarney, his happiness grew. Because his family roots are both in Ireland and Scotland, he was pleased to play both countries. On a day off, walking through a small village, he spotted a tiny guitar in the window of a music store. It was one-quarter the size of the normal instrument. We walked in and Glen toyed with the idea of buying it. I reminded him that he already owned dozens of fine guitars. Besides, we didn't have a case to carry it in. Glen reluctantly agreed, but back in the hotel he turned cranky. He was furious at me. Why did I talk him out of that guitar? He wanted it. He had to have it. I realized it might have reminded him of his first guitar ordered from the Sears catalog when he was a little boy. So I apologized. We went back and bought it.

Don't you know that he never let go of that little guitar. He loved it. He caressed it like a child caresses a teddy bear. I began to see it as his inner child, a part of him that remained pure. I saw that, in refusing to buy it initially, I had been insensitive. What I had seen as a capricious whim was really a healing connection to his past. It didn't make sense to me, but it made sense to Glen. And that's what mattered. I think of myself as a sensitive person, but I learned, through Glen's ever-evolving relationship to memory, that sensitivity, like love, is infinite. Just as love expands, so must sensitivity.

Sensitivity was required by everyone, especially the band's bassist, Siggy Sjursen. Siggy was a fine musician, but Glen found fault with him. Glen's ability to hear high tones had diminished, so the bass always seemed too loud to him. Siggy often became the object of Glen's scorn. As Alzheimer's ate away at Glen's "the show must go on" attitude, his stage manner deteriorated. During actual performances, he started complaining that Siggy's bass was too loud. He became so annoyed that he'd walk over to Siggy during the show, take the bass out of his hands, and tell him to leave the stage. We had to resort to hiding Siggy offstage behind the curtain so he could play without distracting Glen. Ultimately, things got so bad that Siggy graciously bowed out and was replaced by Harry Nilsson's son Kiefo. Knowing the history that preceded him, Kiefo was understandably terrified. But he hung in and performed well. There were moments when, looking over at Kiefo's bass, Glen still complained that Siggy was playing too loud, although Siggy was long gone. It was both funny and sad.

Funny and sad became the description of so much of Glen's behavior. He befriended the filmmakers accompanying us from country to country and city to city, but would often ask me, "Who are those guys? What are they doing?" Then when they weren't with us, he'd say, "Where are my buddies? The guys with the cameras. That film is the most important thing I am doing."

Glen could brush his teeth and carry on a conversation, but minutes later would forget that he'd brushed his teeth or what the conversation had been about. He'd forget that he just performed a show or that there was another show to perform the next night. And yet at that show, the moment he heard Ashley's intro to "Gentle on My Mind," his eyes sparkled like the rhinestones on his Manuel jacket. He was back in full force, and I, along with his appreciative audience, was privileged to behold the celestial marriage of music and memory.

In February 2012, the Grammys planned to honor Glen with a Lifetime Achievement Award. At times he understood the significance, and other times he didn't. He kept asking me what all the fuss was about. The buildup to the big night was intense. Clothier John Varvatos had generously offered to dress Glen for the occasion. I drove him to the Varvatos shop in West Hollywood and was almost there when Glen decided to get out of the car to pee in the middle of traffic. I had to grab him by the arm to keep him from doing just that. He grew angry, and somehow I grew even stronger.

"You are not getting out of this car!" I scolded him like a mother. Though I loathed that role, this was one time when I had to play that part. He could have easily been run over. I kept him from getting out of the car but resolved to always have another person with us whenever we drove.

The Lifetime Achievement Awards were off camera and took place the day before. We sat on the front row with another Lifetime recipient, George Jones. When it was time to accept the award itself, Glen wanted me to accompany him to the podium. I was happy to do it, not because I wanted to share the glory, but because he wanted me at his side, and I feared he couldn't get through the speech without me. My fears were well-grounded.

Glen started off by saying, "I'm left with nothing to say. My tongue's tied for the first time in a long while. My wife tells me I talk too much anyway."

I cued him by saying, "There are some folks you'd like to thank."

"Who?"

I read off the list: the Academy, Stan Schneider, his manager of fifty years.

"Fifty years!" Glen exclaimed. "I ain't that old yet."

The audience howled.

But because Glen couldn't remember anyone else, I named them for him: his children; Bill Maclay, his road manager for thirty-five years; Jimmy Webb; Julian Raymond; the Wrecking Crew; Tommy Smothers, who gave him his first TV show; John Wayne, who put him in *True Grit*.

As I went on, he mimicked me by opening and closing his hand like a puppet and saying, "My wife sure does like to talk."

I didn't mind. The mimicking was funny and the audience loved it.

"Thanks so much," Glen said. "You're all wonderful."

And with that, we were off the stage.

The televised portion of the Grammys is always overstimulating. Stars are everywhere. But that night Glen was cool. We walked the red carpet. He smiled for the cameras. Later that night the Band Perry and Blake Shelton would be performing a tribute to Glen; he would join them at the end to sing "Rhinestone Cowboy." The Grammys are the most-watched musical event in the world, and the broadcast was live. His performance that night was going to be the biggest challenge we had faced thus far. There was so much to distract him, and his teleprompter was not in front of him on the edge of the stage as he was accustomed to, but rather out in the middle of twenty thousand people. We sat behind Katy Perry and in front of Bonnie Raitt until Glen had to go backstage.

Everyone stood on their feet for Glen as Julian escorted him to his microphone. Paul McCartney fist-pumped and sang along as Glen sang "Rhinestone Cowboy." Glen had no idea where the teleprompter was, so he just made up the few lyrics that he couldn't remember. Like the pro that he was, he did it with so much conviction that most people had no idea he had improvised. I have never seen such an outpouring of love and support. The audience applauded a living legend who displayed the vulnerability and innocence of a child and the confidence of a superstar. Everyone admired his courage. No one more than me.

I treasure one special memory of that hectic evening. It happened at the after-party. Glen was given a swag bag of gifts that included a hoodie that read "Music Is My Life." He looked it over, took a black Sharpie, crossed out "Music," and replaced it with "God."

"Ain't that better?" he asked me.

I assured him it was.

The tour went on for nearly two years. Glen played 151 shows. That fact still astounds me. Beyond the flights abroad, the endless bus treks to every corner of the country took their toll. And yet he persisted. Glen was always grateful for his fans. He knew they were the source of not only his material success but his ability to keep his spirit strong. Still there's a huge gulf between fans and eBay vultures. The eBay vultures assaulted us at airports, in hotel lobbies, and at backstage doors in virtually every city. They didn't care about Glen. They cared only about getting their albums and guitars signed so they could sell them on eBay and cash in on Glen's celebrity. I do believe in compassion for all, but I was hardpressed to find compassion for strangers interrupting our dinners or grabbing at Glen the moment he stepped off the bus. Their motives were strictly mercenary, and their actions only served to confuse him. We ultimately found ways to wall ourselves off from the predators, but their ongoing presence trampled our tranquility. Fortunately, the true fans outnumbered the vultures a hundred to one.

CHAPTER 21

POWER AND GLORY FOREVER

I suspect the Goodbye Tour will go down in music history, not just because of the bravery Glen exhibited, the awareness of Alzheimer's he brought to the world, and the lasting connection he made with his friends, but because we were fortunate to document on film what it means to be a real artist.

Glen loved the blues. Among the other genres he had mastered, the blues was one of his favorites. I once heard him quote bluesman Lightnin' Hopkins, who said, "You play the blues to lose the blues." That's what the tour was all about. In spite of the steady deterioration of his memory and mind, in spite of what had to be a ferocious onslaught of the blues, a depression that often accompanies Alzheimer's, Glen played the blues to lose the blues. Onstage, the audience was privileged to watch that miraculous transformation from pain and confusion to clarity and pleasure.

As we traveled, the signs of Glen's deterioration became evident. Sometimes the sign would be obvious. He'd stop in the middle of a show for no reason and wander offstage. Other signs were more subtle. One sign in particular broke my heart.

We were home in Malibu, on break from the tour. During the day, Glen had played golf. That also became a challenge. Though he was a lifelong golfer, the sport he knew so well became confusing. Which club to use? What hole to play? It was only Dante's kind understanding that allowed him to continue. Even when Glen accused Dante of stealing his golf clubs—acute paranoia is another side effect of Alzheimer's—Dante never barked back. He was a loyal and loving friend.

That evening Glen and I got into bed and snuggled. We said goodnight to one another as we had done for thirty years. Then Glen recited the Lord's Prayer.

> Our Father who art in heaven
> Holy is Your Name
> Your kingdom come
> Your will be done
> On earth as it is in heaven

He then fell silent. I sensed what happened. He'd forgotten the rest of the words. I continued to pray out loud for him.

> Give us this day our daily bread
> And forgive us our sins
> As we forgive those who sin against us
> Lead us not into temptation
> But deliver us from evil

He was then able to join me in finishing the prayer with the concluding doxology:

> For Thine is the kingdom
> And the power and the glory forever

Silence followed. I wasn't sure what was going through Glen's mind.

"What's wrong, honey?" I asked.

"I'm afraid."

"Afraid of what?"

"Afraid that I'll forget the prayer."

"I'll always be here to help you," I said.

"Promise me, Kim, that you'll remind me to say the Lord's Prayer every day. It's the one thing I don't want to forget."

I promised, but I knew that eventually he would forget the prayer. He would eventually forget everything. It was a sobering moment. I say that because it made me realize that, in addition to fighting to retain his memory, Glen was fighting to retain his closeness to God.

Another moment came in the spring of 2012. We had an extra day off while traveling through Michigan, so we stopped at a quaint little bed and breakfast on Lake Erie to spend the night. We arrived just in time for dinner, and we were all starving, so Bill offered to wait for the restaurant to open to get a table big enough for our entourage. He invited Glen to wait with him while I put our things in the room.

There was a little gift shop right next to the restaurant with a sign out front that read, "Mother's Day." Glen's eyes opened wide as he read the sign out loud. "Mother's Day! I want to buy Kim a present." Bill said. "Well, maybe we can find something in the gift shop. Let's look." Glen started walking up and down the aisles. "Pink," Glen thought out loud, "Kim loves pink! I want to buy her something pink." I had just made my way downstairs and saw Glen at the register getting ready to buy me something *very* pink, a large bottle of Pepto-Bismol. I immediately intervened.

"We don't need that, Glen," I said, seeing it as an impulsive purchase. Compulsive purchases were becoming more common. I put the bottle back on the shelf.

During dinner that night, Bill leaned across the table and whispered, "Glen saw the sign saying that it was Mother's Day and wanted to surprise you by giving you something pink." My jaw dropped. I had no idea. Tears filled my eyes. A wave of loving gratitude washed over me. That would have been the most heartfelt gift he would have ever given me. My dismissive action robbed him of a chance to express his love. It also robbed me of receiving that love. The episode humbled me, reminding me of my obligation—to take the time to try to understand what might be on Glen's mind. Alzheimer's is a mysterious disease, but its mysteries do not mean we can't look for signs of love.

There were other signs I never expected. Glen became fascinated with colors. Every time he saw a blue car, he shouted, "That's gonna be my next car. It's gonna be bright blue." At a truck stop, he bought a NASCAR jacket covered with colorful logos that transformed Glen into a walking billboard for every brand from Kobalt tools to Top Choice Lumber. He wouldn't take the jacket off for weeks. He even wanted to wear it onstage. I probably should have let him—what difference would it have made?—but I argued that the fans had come to see a show and wanted to see him in his show clothes. He conceded, but the second the show was over, he put on the NASCAR jacket and wore it to bed.

Jane Seymour, a woman of rare insight, saw Glen's affinity for bright colors and took him into her art studio and urged him to paint. At first he was hesitant but soon got into it. Jane suggested that he look for the rhythm in painting. She assured him there were no mistakes. Just like that, Glen put palette knife and brush to canvas, singing "Rhinestone Cowboy" and "Am I Blue" as he worked. He became focused and lighthearted. He actually created two paintings, naming one *An Old House* and the other *Am I Blue*. He also did a mixed-media collage, drawing a guitar over a board pasted over with his old CD covers. (See "The Art of Glen Campbell" on Facebook.)

Early on, the doctors had told me about the healing impact of music as an exceptional creative experience for dementia and Alzheimer's patients. Jane had shown how art could provide a similar experience.

We made an important stop in Washington, DC. After a show at the Library of Congress, we took out two days to meet with senators and representatives to advocate for Alzheimer's research. The highlight of the visit was Ashley testifying for a congressional committee. As she spoke, our daughter fought back tears.

"As our nation's leaders," she said, "I respectfully ask that you support the implementation of the national Alzheimer's plan and that you fund the president's budget request of an additional $100 million for Alzheimer's this year. In my family, music was always a part of our home, and we are still playing. We knew at the beginning that Alzheimer's doesn't rob you of the things you love right away, but the disease will keep getting worse and there aren't any medications today that can stop it. Alzheimer's is a disease that robs people of their lives while they are still living them, and it robs families of the people they love while they are still standing in front of their eyes. I think a person's life is comprised of memories, and that's exactly what this disease takes away from you. Like the memory of my dad taking me fishing in Flagstaff when I was a little girl. Or playing banjo with my dad while he played guitar. Now when I play banjo with my dad, it's getting harder for him to follow along, and it's getting harder for him to recall my name. It's hard to come to the realization that someday my dad might look at me, and I will be absolutely nothing to him. We need to find a cure for this because we are not the only family affected. So much pain should not exist in the world. Let's work together to end Alzheimer's."

At that time, $400 million was being spent on all neurological diseases per year. I'm glad to report that in 2019 the National Institute of Health is expected to spend $3.08 billion on Alzheimer's research alone.

Winding our way back across the country, we did a show at the Hollywood Bowl, billed as Glen's final concert in Los Angeles. Jackson Browne, Lucinda Williams, and Kris Kristofferson all gave moving tributes. *Rolling Stone* raved, pointing to Glen's "still-strong singing" and "tasty guitar solos." The reviewer spoke of the "almost unbearable poignancy of a man delivering old lyrics heavy with new meaning, as when he admitted, in 'Galveston,' I'm so afraid of dying."

On the other coast, in another historic cultural setting, he played Carnegie Hall. A group of us went out walking in Times Square. We stopped at Starbucks for a coffee. I said I was running across the street to Capezio to buy dancewear. While I was gone, Glen somehow slipped out of the Starbucks while no one was looking. Panic set in. The group split up in five different directions. Times Square was a kaleidoscope of neon. Taxis, tourists, a mad scramble of humanity. Where's Waldo? How to find Glen? Fortunately, Glen was wearing a bright blue beanie, which our grandson Jesse Olson spotted.

"Hey, Grandpa," he said, "where you going?"

"Oh, I just saw a blue car and wanted to get a better look."

Jesse saved the day. But then came the night. Before the big show at Carnegie Hall, Glen took a nice long nap. When it was time to get ready for the show, he refused to get up. He didn't care that we were in New York. He didn't care that we were about to play the world's most prestigious venue. Nothing would move him. I called our security man Clancy to see if his son, whom Glen called Whistle Britches, could help convince Glen to get up. When I prompted the boy to ask Glen to do his Donald Duck imitation, Glen jumped out of bed and turned into Donald. He was off and running. Into the shower. Into his show clothes. And then to the stage, where his performance was superb. One critic quoted Glen's favorite joke about his condition. "I can still jump as high but just can't stay up long." Glen made it clear, added the critic, "there wasn't a place in the world he'd rather be than onstage." The critic was right.

Deterioration was inevitable, yet that didn't make it less painful. During one show Glen was distracted by the air-conditioning, stopped singing, and asked for a jacket. During another show, he simply stopped singing and asked out loud where he was and what he was doing. The audiences were invariably beautiful. Seeing the breakdown in his behavior, they simply applauded wildly until he started singing again.

On November 30, 2012, we were in Napa, California,

scheduled to play the Uptown Theater. The wine country was in full bloom. The band and crew planned to visit a winery in the afternoon. I rarely got to see anything but the inside of a hotel room because my job was to care for Glen. I cherished that job, but I had never been to Napa and really wanted to explore. Thankfully, Dante and his wife, Brody, had driven up from Malibu to see the show, so later that afternoon Dante said he'd be happy to take Glen for a walk. This was my chance to see a little of the charming town with Brody. Unfortunately, I had forgotten to tell Dante not to take Glen to the theater. Sound checks easily set him off. Too late! It was not long before I got a desperate phone call from Bill begging me to come and get Glen.

He had taken over the sound check and was upset and agitated about the sound of the bass. He was ranting and raving and firing everyone. When I arrived, I'd never seen him this furious at his musicians. Somehow, I managed to get him back to the hotel, showered, and dressed in time for the show.

For the most part, that show was a disaster. During his guitar solo on "Gentle on My Mind," he complained the sound was too thin and, in protest, played bad notes and dissonant chords. He ruined the song. His agitation grew from there. The only respite was when he looked at the teleprompter for the next song and the title puzzled him.

"'A Better Place,'" he said. "Who wrote that?"

"You did, Daddy," answered Ashley.

"That's my baby girl," he said. "The best woman banjo player around."

Ashley often was able to defuse him, but after singing "A Better Place," he grew angry again. He fired the band three times before launching into "Try a Little Tenderness." The irony of his screaming at his band followed by a plea for tenderness was not lost on him. He threw up his hands and apologized to the band, and the audience and laughed at the absurdity of it all. Everyone onstage smiled, and the audience stood on their feet and cheered him. They were cheering his past triumphs but also his present courage. They knew he didn't have to be there. But he was. He was still in the mix. He was still Glen Campbell.

The Napa show convinced us that the party was over. The agony and ecstasy had come to an end. Time to pack it up and head home. The doctors confirmed what I already knew. Glen had slipped into the late stages of Alzheimer's.

CHAPTER 22

DEEP SECLUSION

A friend read me a poem by William Wordsworth written at the end of the eighteenth century, commonly known as "Tintern Abbey."

> Five years have passed; five summers, with the length
> Of five long winters! and again I hear
> These waters, rolling from their mountain-springs
> With a soft inland murmur.—Once again
> Do I behold these steep and lofty cliffs,
> That on a wild secluded scene impress
> Thoughts of more deep seclusion; and connect
> The landscape with the quiet of the sky.

I quote these lines not only because of their lyrical beauty, but because five years is the approximate length of time Glen suffered with the final and most trying period of Alzheimer's. It was during these five years that I looked to nature for sustenance. The ocean. The flowers. The sun, the moon, the stars. And God. Always God.

Becoming a caregiver of an Alzheimer's patient can be dangerous. The caregiver—at least this caregiver—runs the risk of serious depression. Thus I sought solace wherever I could find it. The sermons and books of Joel Osteen helped enormously. I found his message uplifting and unfalteringly positive. Joyce

Meyer too. Her admonitions to "trust God and do good" when you don't know what else to do helped me put one foot in front of the other. I danced as often as I could. I prayed continually. I leaned on my children for support as they leaned on me. I reached out to friends.

The late stages of our journey with Alzheimer's were rife with drama. In conveying that drama, I want to be judicious. If I were to list every bizarre behavior or incident, I would be doing no one any favors, either myself or Glen. At the same time, to expose the nature of the disease requires the inclusion of certain details.

I felt like I was living in a loop. The movie *Groundhog Day* comes to mind. It felt like I was living the same day over and over, answering the same questions, going through the same routines. Embracing victimization is never helpful, and I fought against that tendency. Instead of seeing each day as drudgery, I prayed each morning for gratitude. *Thank you, God, for allowing me to honor my husband in the most meaningful way possible, to love him in sickness and in health.* I pushed aside my own pain, hugged him, reassured him, and dug down ever deeper for a little more tenderness.

A big boost was connecting to other caregivers across the country. I became an energetic advocate in raising funds for a cure. I read, listened to lectures, and, of course, danced whenever I had the chance.

Glen grew more solemn. He couldn't watch TV because he couldn't follow a storyline or even understand a sports match. He couldn't read a book. He was frustrated and bored. He brought out twenty of his vintage guitars, took them out of their cases, and then agonized because he couldn't figure out which guitars belonged in which cases. When the UPS man or gardener came to the door, he offered to give them one of the guitars, an instrument that might be priceless. I bolted the guitar closet, but that agitated him even more. He rummaged through every drawer, closet, and cabinet in the house, overturning everything, in search of, well, he could never remember what he was looking for. I managed to distract him by displaying his brightly colored collection of golf caps on a hat tree. He spent weeks taking them off the tree, lining them on the bed, counting them, and reading each one out loud: Malibu Country Club, Tahina, Bob Hope, US Open, St. Andrews, Pebble Beach. He liked all of them so much it was hard for him to decide which one to wear, so rather than making such a hard choice, he decided to wear as many as possible all at once. Humor, as always, helped. When he walked into the kitchen with five golf caps on his head, everyone laughed. Glen was smiling. During those days, a single smile was all I needed.

Most of Glen's golf buddies no longer had the patience to play with Glen. Only Dante, the golf angel, remained his faithful friend. Strangely enough, as the disease progressed, Glen became more interested in finding lost balls in the bushes than playing the game. He would come home each day with his pockets absolutely bulging with balls and wearing a huge smile of accomplishment on his face. One day they brought home seventy-five balls and Dante brought home a bad case of poison oak. Glen spent many hours writing messages on them so that if lost again, whoever found them would read his messages:

God is love.
Love the Lord.
Peace and happiness.
God loves you.

Then his paranoia deepened. It centered on golf. The notion of his friends stealing his clubs never left his mind. He asked for his guns. When I told him we didn't have them anymore, he asked for a wrench to keep in his pocket. This really worried me! Was Glen actually plotting to attack someone?

Help came in the person of Steve Ozark, who had worked as the wardrobe manager for the *Glen Campbell Goodtime Hour* when he was eighteen. He went on to settle in Hawaii, where he became a renowned caterer for everyone from Elton John to Bruno Mars. He offered to stay with us for a while to help care for Glen. We quickly said yes. We've never eaten so well, before or since.

Steve and our nephew Matt kept a watchful eye on Glen, who was always walking the perimeter of our property, looking to climb over the fence. He was forever on the prowl, searching to escape a state of mind that was inescapable.

After one of Steve's sumptuous dinners, Glen rested on the sofa while I washed the dishes and cleaned up. Afterward, I walked over to him.

"Come on, honey," I said. "Let's go up to bed."

He looked at me with a puzzled stare.

"Who are you?" he asked.

My heart sank. That had never happened before.

"It's me, honey!" I said with a lump in my throat.

"I know it's you . . . but who are you?" he asked again.

I drew closer to his face to make sure that he could see me clearly, "It's me, Kim. Your wife. It's time to go to bed now."

I took him by the hand and he reluctantly followed me, still in a state of confusion. When we got to the bottom of the stairs, he gasped as if a light bulb had just been turned on, "Oh! Of course.

You're my darling angel." For a few moments he was lucid. He pulled me to his chest and bit his lower lip as if he were about to burst into tears and said, "Thank you for being my wife and for taking such good care of me." His words broke my heart. We embraced as if we were breathing each other in maybe for the last time. We kissed and said "I love you." As we climbed the stairs together to our room, I wondered if this was our last goodbye. My eyes welled up with tears, but I could not allow myself to linger for more than a moment in that emotionally raw space. The implications of Glen forgetting who I was, was almost too much for me to stand.

I was left with the undeniable fact that we were now in new territory. In our bedroom, I placed a group of noisy plastic hangers on the door as a fail-safe alarm. Should Glen get up in the middle of the night and try to leave the room, I'd be alerted. After undressing him and slipping into my nightgown, I climbed into bed and built a wall of pillows between us to protect myself from an occasional flailing arm or physical response to a bad dream. A few nights earlier he had sat up at 4 a.m. and attacked me with a series of punches. I could only assume he was reacting to a nightmare.

On this night, as he drifted off to sleep, he shouted my name.

"What's wrong?" I asked.

"The floor is missing. The floor is gone."

A shadow had given him the impression of a hole. I stood up to show him that everything was okay; the floor was there. From then on, I kept a night-light by the side of his bed to eliminate shadows.

The sad irony is that just as Glen was losing all memory, I was losing memory of who he was before the disease. That's because

Alzheimer's comes on so gradually that it insidiously impedes your memory of your loved one in his pre-Alzheimer's state. Alzheimer's was effectively robbing both of us of our memories.

Friends urged me to hire in-home help. I wish I could have. Great services are available, but such services were untenable for me. Glen would not react well to professional helpers. He wouldn't understand their purpose. He'd resent their presence and things would only grow worse. His suspicions of strangers had gotten out of hand. I couldn't let him answer the front door for fear of how he might react to anyone standing there.

At times, he couldn't stand being in the house, couldn't stand the confinement, couldn't stand his mental state that was far beyond his comprehension. He was at war with an invisible and inaudible enemy.

I was convinced a major move, while no cure, might give us all a reprieve. I was right, and I was also wrong.

CHAPTER 23

MUSIC CITY

ll right!" Glen enthused when I first mentioned the idea of moving to Nashville. He seemed happy. He had friends galore in Nashville and a music community that adored him. Malibu is idyllic but somewhat isolating. Like Glen, Nashville is far more down-home.

My own reasons for the move involved family. Ashley and Shannon had signed a publishing deal with Warner Chappell and moved there. They were busy writing but missed us as much as we missed them. They realized that, in dealing with Glen, I'd need greater help.

With Ashley and Shannon gone, I relied heavily on Cal. When I took my ballet lessons in Agoura Hills, I'd drop Glen off with Cal, who lived nearby. Once, while Cal was in the back of his place, Glen slipped out the front door and disappeared. Cal went looking for him, finally finding him at the very moment Glen was about to climb into the window of a stranger's house. He had forgotten where Cal lived. He had also forgotten that the way to enter a house is through the front door. Our life in Malibu had grown increasingly unmanageable.

Another huge benefit was Nashville's proximity to Arkansas. The drive was only six hours. That meant more family visits, always a plus. An additional plus was Matt's decision to make the move with us. It didn't take long to find a suitable house, but before the trucks arrived, the packing process had turned difficult. Whatever we packed, Glen immediately unpacked. When he unpacked a heavy Lalique crystal dove that my dad had given us as a wedding gift, I tried to take it from him and, in doing so, it fell to the floor and broke. I lost my cool and scolded Glen. Silently, I scolded myself for scolding him. I went to bed praying for patience. But as a friend likes to say, just when you think you've been patient enough, more patience is required. Like true love, true patience is infinite.

On the flight to Nashville, Glen was disoriented. He tried opening the window next to his seat. Fortunately, we were not in an exit aisle. As we were landing, he jumped up and headed for the bathroom. I couldn't stop him. The attendants were alarmed. I somehow got him back in his seat seconds before the wheels touched down.

Ashley picked us up at the airport and was shocked by her father's deterioration. I was just grateful that he recognized her. His daughter Kelli took him to Delight, Arkansas, to be with his siblings, while I received the furniture and got our house in order.

The skills I gained studying interior decoration at UCLA came in handy. I entered our new house in my ARCHICAD program, creating a 3D model that allowed me to see where to place each piece of furniture and where to install child locks to protect Glen from harm. The front doors were bolted and gates and fences built to enclose the property. I felt like I was setting up a ward. Within a week, everything had been installed.

His sister Sandy called saying he was ready to come to Nashville. She reported some good times, the whole family singing songs, telling stories, and cooking their beloved brother's favorite foods. The only problem was that he'd refused to shower for a week.

By December 2013, we were moved in. The three-bedroom main house had an open floor plan that let me monitor Glen's whereabouts. There was a lower level with a den and three additional bedrooms. I was blessed that Ashley, her college friend Amanda, Shannon, and Matt all moved in. They were there for me every step of the way.

I was Glen's primary caregiver. I'd also take the night shift because I slept with Glen—or should say tried to sleep with Glen. He was up and down, sometimes making it to the bathroom on time, sometimes not. I was painfully aware that my team consisted of young adults in their midtwenties who were voluntarily committing to shoulder immense responsibility at a time they could well have been focusing on their own lives and careers.

The good times were not entirely over. TK Kimbrell and his wife, Laura, hosted music parties at their home, where artists like Toby Keith and Lee Ann Womack came to be with Glen, who enjoyed being the center of attention. He could still play a little guitar.

We hosted a Christmas Eve party to celebrate our new life in Nashville. I spent all day cooking, while Glen's album *That Christmas Feeling* stayed on heavy rotation. Glen loved icing the gingerbread men, but when my back was turned started unwrapping all the presents. I let him. No more scolding. The smell of spiced cider permeated the house. When the guests arrived, though, Glen was inhospitable. He wandered off and wouldn't speak to anyone. Then Ashley brought out her banjo and, once again, the magic of music did the trick. Glen picked up his guitar and played flawlessly. Within seconds, he went from sullen to serene. He sang, laughed, and socialized as though he were the healthiest man alive. A Christmas miracle.

TK and Laura invited us to Richland Country Club for New Year's Eve. Glen looked dashing in his black cashmere jacket. As guests trickled in, everyone wanted to meet him. He did well with his auto-reply small talk. He didn't understand everything being said to him, but he maintained his composure. After dinner, we girls hit the dance floor. When the song, "My Girl" began to play, Glen decided he wanted to dance, too, and made his way to the floor. Ashley took the first half of the song and I took the second. When that song ended, the band began to play "Unforgettable." It was as if God had created the soundtrack for the evening. Like the Red Sea, the room parted as Glen took his daughter in his arms, and, as though he understood the irony of the lyrics—and perhaps he did—he danced with gentle grace. There wasn't a dry eye in the room. Ashley has that father-daughter dance to remember when she gets married one day.

Unforgettable in every way
And forever more, that's how you'll stay
That's why, darling, it's incredible
That someone so unforgettable
Thinks that I'm unforgettable too

When the clock struck midnight, Glen was still smiling. He took my hand, kissed my lips, and pledged his love. The memory is unforgettable.

On Monday nights Ashley liked to sit in with Carl Jackson to play an old-school country music show at a venue in the Gulch called Station Inn. Because music had worked so well for Glen over the holidays, we decided to take Glen to the show. The little stone building looked like a relic from the past juxtaposed against the swank high-rise hotels, condos, fashion boutiques, and trend-setting restaurants of one of Nashville's hottest neighborhoods. The interior reflected the austerity of the exterior. (Spoiler alert: if you go to the ladies' room at Station Inn, be prepared to do your business behind a curtain made from a flour sack rather than a stall door.)

As I looked around the room at the posters of Minnie Pearl, Merle Haggard, and Boxcar Willie, a wave of nostalgia washed over me. I was awestruck that my husband was part of that rich history. All eyes were on us as we sat down at a table reserved for us at the edge of the stage. Carl had been a part of our family since he fixed Glen and me up on that blind date in 1981. My hope was that Glen would be able to remember and connect with Carl, who opened the show, saying, "For many years, I've had the privilege of being the banjo player for that man right over there, Glen Campbell, an American musical treasure." The audience acknowledged Glen, but Glen looked confused. Not long into Carl's set, Glen turned to me and said, "Well, this is a waste of time. Where's the food?" He raised his voice and grew incensed that no food was in front of him. I realized that he thought he was in a restaurant and ordered him a microwaved pizza. That's what they serve there. Microwaved pizza saved the day.

After the show Carl came over to hug Glen and asked him how he liked the show. I laughed to myself because I knew what Glen *would* have jested if he had his memory: *"Carl, you always cease to amaze me."* When I shared what Glen had actually said to me during the show, Carl just about fell on the floor laughing. Glen didn't know why Carl was laughing, but he liked to make people laugh and proudly took credit for it. Pretty soon we were all laughing. What else can you do? Glen said in the documentary, "I've laughed and I've cried, and laughing is a whole lot better."

On another night, Ashley and Shannon were playing a show at a small venue called the Basement. I decided to take Glen to see our kids perform. People seemed in awe that Glen Campbell was in the building. We sat at a small table right in front. I could tell he was proud of our kids. Then Ashley introduced their final song for the evening:

"We'd like to end with a song that I wrote for my dad who has Alzheimer's. I wanted to describe the relationship swap I was experiencing going from my father taking care of me to me taking care of my father. I wanted to have something that could reach him when memory and words failed, and that's definitely music. So this is a song from me to him, letting him know that I'll always have his back. It's called 'Remembering.'"

A hush of reverence enveloped the room as Ashley sang to her father.

Four years old running up the stairs to your bed
Thunder rolls and I pull the covers over my head
You say it's just a storm, enjoy the show
You take me to the window, and you show me that it's beautiful
Never had to ask you to sing for me, it's
just the way you put me at ease

Bone for bone we are the same
Bones get tired and they can't carry all the weight

We can talk until you can't even remember my name
Daddy don't you worry, I'll do the remembering

First guitar and I just wasn't getting it right
You showed me how to play it, said
it doesn't happen overnight
And in a couple years I come home and
show you how I play "Blackbird"
And though I miss a couple notes you still
say that it was the best you ever heard
Never had to ask you to smile for me, it's
just the way you put me at ease

Bone for bone we are the same
Bones get tired and they can't carry all the weight
We can talk until you can't even remember my name
Daddy don't you worry, I'll do the remembering

Now I have to ask you to sing for me
And I have to show you the words to sing
You're standing right in front of me and slipping away

Bone for bone we are the same
Bones get tired and they can't carry all the weight
We can talk until you can't even remember my name
Daddy don't you worry, I'll do the remembering

After the song was sung, silence. The silence lingered a long while. And then Glen stood up and shouted, "Hey, that was good!" The room went wild with applause.

CHAPTER 24

THE PELL-MELL BELL

In January 2014, I made a decision not to take Glen out in public. It was too confusing and stressful for him. He looked disheveled. His eyes were glazed over. I didn't want people to see or photograph him. He became a shut-in, and I became a shut-in with him.

It was impossible to get a full night's sleep with Glen beside me, so I asked the team for help. They understood that I couldn't afford to fall apart. We divided up the night watch. We installed motion detectors and monitors to track his wanderings. If he got out of bed or up out of a chair, an alarm sounded. That sound dominated the house. We call it the pell-mell bell because when it rang we all ran pell-mell to make sure Glen got to the bathroom before it was too late. Most of the time it was too late. The pell-mell bell ran almost incessantly. It got so bad that all we could do was laugh about it. But the laughing didn't last long. We all began crumbling under the anxious weight of waiting for the next disaster. He might be eating a box of Kleenex or autographing the walls with a magic marker or pulling dishes out onto the floor. He wouldn't bathe or change clothes.

My research about the disease never ceased. In David Shenk's book, *The Forgetting*, he writes of "caregiver's dementia." My team and I were experiencing just that, a form of depression during which our lives were controlled by Glen's every whim. Our hearts were also breaking. We were witnessing Glen's final demise.

Most of the time Glen was as gentle and sweet as he could be, but other times he became combative. When I tried to get him in the shower, he'd raise his fist to threaten me. If I persisted, he'd twist my arm behind my back so hard I thought it'd break. My response was always the same, "Okay, sweetie. I'm sorry. Please let me go. I love you." He'd always released me, but I worried the next time he might not.

His diminishing ability to reason and comprehend language made any effort to correct him potentially dangerous. Once when I found him drinking milk from a carton and offered him a glass, he gave me a sinister look and tried to knee me in the stomach. Seconds later, he was lovey dovey.

His aggression was increasingly unpredictable. One afternoon he picked up a large butcher knife from the cutting board and pointed it at me in a threatening manner. I felt like Dudley Moore's character in the movie *Arthur* when his fiancée's father, angry with Arthur for leaving his daughter at the altar, picked up a knife and walked toward him with madness in his eyes. To which Arthur hopefully queried, "Do you think he wants some cheese?"

Glen's doctor had prescribed a number of medicinal cocktails to help Glen sleep and curb his agitation, but nothing helped. I feared for his safety as well as my own and that of my team. I decided it was time to find a neurologist in Nashville who could help monitor Glen's progression and oversee his medications.

I took Glen to Vanderbilt University Medical Center for what I assumed would be a routine appointment. When the doctor asked Glen where he was, he just stared at his feet. I wasn't surprised that he could not answer his questions or that it took an hour of coaxing before he would allow the nurse to draw his blood. It had taken us almost that long to get him in the car for the drive over.

After all of the tests had been concluded, the neurologist took me aside. "Mrs. Campbell, from what I've seen today and from what you've told me about his behavior, I can't believe you're still trying to manage this at home. It's clearly not safe for him, you, or your team. I'm going to have a social worker contact you."

I felt stunned. Objections rushed to mind. The doctor didn't understand—couldn't understand! Who knew Glen better than I did, his wife of thirty-one years? He needed to be close to me. Had we not solemnly promised each other "for better or for worse, in sickness and in health, for richer or poorer?" To even think about moving Glen out of the home felt like a breach of our marriage vows.

By then I was in crisis. I decided to educate myself about what resources might be out there. The social worker put me in touch with an expert in memory care. The expert told me about in-home care, day care, respite care and residential care. I told her that I had no interest in placing Glen in a nursing home. Nursing homes, she said, were for people requiring round-the-clock *skilled* nursing, not necessarily for people with dementia. Memory care communities, however, were specifically designed for those with cognitive impairment. Such professional communities provide safe and secure environments with 24/7 access to medical care. They strive to help each patient maintain their identity, dignity, and autonomy as much as possible, while respecting their history and hobbies. They offer therapies designed to stimulate memory and provide a means for patients to express themselves through art and music. Physically, they have the look of a real home or fine hotel. Fellowship and socialization, I was told, is vital for people with Alzheimer's. I was shocked. I didn't know that such places even existed.

And yet I still resisted. I couldn't imagine Glen apart from me. Beyond that, his Alzheimer's was so advanced I couldn't picture him participating in joint activities. But common sense said that I needed to learn more. I needed to see for myself. I asked my friend Lynn to watch Glen while my team and I checked out a few of these communities. One excursion lasted less than a half-hour. Lynn called, saying, "Kim, he's freaking out, and I don't know what to do. He's hyperventilating, running around, pulling on doors, trying to take his clothes off. I'm afraid if he's able to open the front door, I won't be able to stop him from running away."

We rushed home to take over. It turned out that Glen needed to use the bathroom and couldn't find it. When I got him in the bathroom, he kept looking at the shower. I kept pointing at the toilet, but he'd forgotten how to use it. In trying to help him, he took a swing at me. I ducked in time. Now I knew what I had known weeks earlier but was not willing to admit: neither I nor my devoted team could handle Glen.

It was March 4, 2014. After visiting multiple memory care communities, I finally found a place that reminded me of some of the nice hotels we stayed in during our tour. The community sat on a hill surrounded by a rolling lawn and lush flower gardens. It had an open floor plan with a central kitchen that made it feel like home. After much prayer, I made the painful decision to try adult daycare. My eyes welled with tears as I filled out the paperwork.

It seemed surreal to be taking my husband, who was twenty-two years my senior, to his first day of daycare. The drive brought a change in scenery. The narrow streets lined with homes and businesses opened to a quiet road that made its way through wild grasses and majestic trees, still glistening with the slowly melting ice of a winter that had long overstayed its welcome. For some reason, Glen remained calm in the car on the way there. Everything usually went smoother in the mornings. As we pulled up to the community, Glen pressed his face to the window, entranced by the sight of geese floating on the placid waters of an enormous pond. I tried to imagine what he felt experiencing the beauty of God's creation as if for the very first time in his life. The whole world was new to him—every day. I worried that he would experience separation anxiety when I left and that he might become disoriented, confused, or afraid. I was riddled with fear that he might become angry with me for bringing him there. I thought it would be a good idea to leave him with something familiar that might distract him or comfort him, so I filled his pockets with guitar picks and brought along the child-sized guitar we'd bought in Ireland.

As the strong wooden doors of the memory community opened, we were showered with a warm and welcoming light. Much to my surprise, the minute Glen walked in he started smiling, shaking hands, and handing out guitar picks as if he was at a meet and greet before a show. He loved being around people and making them smile.

They took us upstairs to a living room appointed with cozy club chairs and a long leather sofa facing a beautiful stone fireplace. The room commanded a splendid view of the Tennessee hills through a large picture window. A care partner took Glen for a walk to show him around.

The staff assured me everything would be fine. Ashley, Matt, and I went home, not knowing what to think or how to feel. We just sat around the kitchen table for a while, absorbed in our own thoughts. I felt absolutely stunned that we were taking a step like this. The house felt strangely quiet. I was extremely depressed and just laid my head down on the table and wept.

When 4:30 p.m. came around, we drove back to the community in silence as I braced myself for the worst. I worried I might find Glen seething with anger, feeling that I had abandoned him. I imagined him frightened and disoriented, searching for me. Then another fear struck me. What if he does not remember me? I knew that day would come, but what if leaving him in a foreign environment without me snapped the last threads on which his ability to recognize me hung? I decided *that* would be worse than him being angry at me.

When we arrived to pick him up, I went into the clubroom to find Glen sitting at the kitchen bar with a care partner, flipping through a cookbook. He was completely at ease. I had not seen him focus on a book in a long time. He seemed so content. I wondered how she did it.

I asked how his day went. "Right after you left, Glen took his little guitar and stood up in front of the residents in the living room. He played them a few songs, and then took a big bow and thanked them all for coming. Then he laid down on the sofa and took a nice long nap. He had a good day."

His positive experience that day, though, did not last. At home, he grew agitated and belligerent. I'd read enough to know that Alzheimer's can cause "sundowning," a term that describes symptoms that occur in late afternoon and into the night, causing confusion and aggression. The cause is unknown, but the triggers are low lighting and shadows.

We were back to dealing with Glen during the most difficult hours, 10:00 p.m. to morning. We were back to our shifts, back to the sound of the pell-mell bell. At one point, Ashley began silently weeping. "I'm already twenty-seven and still living at home," she said. Her words broke my heart. She felt guilty and selfish for harboring such thoughts, and I felt guilty and selfish when I considered what I was asking her to sacrifice for Glen and me. She had set aside her own hopes and dreams out of loyalty to her parents. She embodied the Bible's injunction to honor your father and your mother, and she did not regret that choice, but at the same time she could never get those years back.

That first day of daycare and the horrific nights that followed at home convinced me of a truth I had so resisted. Glen needed round-the-clock medical care. As an interim move, Glen would move into the community for two weeks. Then we'd reevaluate. We packed his bag, made sure to include photos and a guitar, and drove over. On the way, I thought of the lyrics of the song that Glen and Julian Raymond had written for the soundtrack of our documentary, "The Long Walk Home." The lyrics reassured me that our love would carry us on to our final destination.

Some familiar place I've never been before
This is a long walk home
A beautiful feeling like I've never known
This is a long walk home

I know I'll never be the same again
I hope I'll still remember you
Above it all I know our love will transcend
On my long walk home

No more places that I need to be
This is the long walk home
No more people tryin' to get at me
This is the long walk home

Whatever will be will be my friend
No more fences on that line to mend
It's the only debt I've never paid that I owed
This is the long walk home

Glen enjoyed shaking hands and meeting everyone for the first time, again. He liked hanging with the other residents. There was one man in particular he spent time conversing with. None of what they said made sense, but it seemed meaningful to them.

He settled into his room without complaints, and we said goodbye. We went back home emotionally spent. We all sat around the kitchen table in a stupor, staring at each other in disbelief. There was not much to say. Alzheimer's had almost completely consumed us. As I struggled with a heavy load of guilt, I continued to weigh the situation in my mind. I thought about the doctor's advice and the fact that he knew more about what lay ahead with this disease than I did. *Besides,* I said to myself, *what if this is actually good for Glen?* I found comfort knowing that we could bring Glen back and forth as much as we wanted. If it wasn't working out, we could always bring him back home to stay.

Nevertheless, we all had an immense sense of loss and sorrow. Feeling the need to get out of the house, we went to hear Carl Jackson at the Station Inn. Shannon got up and sang. He looked and sounded so much like Glen it brought tears to my eyes. Then

Carl called Ashley up to the stage. She glowed proudly when he hugged her and introduced her as Glen's daughter and his goddaughter. Carl told some funny stories about traveling with Glen, and soon we were all laughing through our tears. It felt like Glen was right there with us.

When we returned home, Ashley said, "Mom, I've decided *not* to feel guilty for being happy." Then it hit me. I knew with absolute certainty that Glen would never want his daughter to feel *guilty* for being happy. He would want her to enjoy her life, pursue her dreams, blossom, and flourish. He would never want any of us to become another victim of this disease.

During this trial period, I spent so much time with Glen he thought I lived there too. "Where's your room?" he kept asking.

"This is *our* room, honey," I said. "We're here together."

Because real communication was no longer possible, Glen and I communicated mostly with smiles, hugs, and walks in the garden. I felt alone but made sure that he did not. I felt like I was holding his hand on earth and God was holding his hand in heaven. The title song of *Ghost on the Canvas* haunted me:

I know a place between life and death for you and me
Best take hold on the threshold of eternity
And see the ghost on the canvas
People don't see us
Ghost on the canvas
People don't know
When they're looking at soul.

The twinkle in his eye let me know that his soul was still there with me. Yet I felt completely alone. I missed his mind. I missed my best friend, my lover, my husband, my protector. I felt vulnerable. I was barely treading water in a sea of depression.

The one thing that saved me from sinking any further was the release in April 2014 of *Glen Campbell: I'll Be Me*, the film that documented the Goodbye Tour. It premiered at the Nashville Film Festival and proved a roaring success. Fans and critics were virtually unanimous in feeling how the film captured Glen's courage, honesty, and vulnerability.

A day later I threw a private party at the Country Music Hall of Fame to celebrate Glen's seventy-eighth birthday. I had pledged not to take Glen out in public but made an exception because the museum was closed and this gathering would consist only of close friends. I didn't have to worry about anyone taking pictures and selling them to the paparazzi.

On the drive from the memory community to the hall, he panicked. He started crying, trying to take his shirt off and beating on the windows. We turned up the car radio hoping that music might calm him down. It did not. We were four miles into an eight-mile drive, so there was no turning back. It was painful to see Glen so distressed. Once we arrived, we immediately took him to the bathroom. After that, he calmed down and was composed enough to walk through the Hall with us. Display cases were filled with Glen's memorabilia, but it wasn't the old posters and albums that interested him. It was the glass in which the objects were encased. He kept examining the glass, never noticing what was on display behind it.

What he did notice was a big chocolate birthday cake with "GLEN" on top. Once he spied the cake, we could not make him wait. We all sang "Happy Birthday" and cut him a big slice.

Everyone relished embracing Glen that night, knowing that it might be their last opportunity to say goodbye.

Goodbye, goodbye . . . Alzheimer's is a journey filled with last goodbyes, and every one of them is heartbreaking.

The eventual nationwide release of *I'll Be Me* generated even more enthusiasm. It brought Alzheimer's out of the shadows and opened up a national conversation. Millions of people suddenly felt seen and heard because we were telling their story too. The film's success gave me a platform to advocate for people with dementia and their families. I soon found that helping others helped me cope with my pain and loneliness.

It wasn't long before we heard the news that a song Julian and Glen wrote for the film, "I'm Not Gonna Miss You," had been nominated for both a Grammy and Oscar.

I'm still here, but yet I'm gone
I don't play guitar or sing my songs
They never defined who I am
The man that loves you 'til the end

You're the last person I will love
You're the last face I will recall
And best of all, I'm not gonna miss you
Not gonna miss you

I'm never gonna hold you like I did
Or say I love you to the kids
You're never gonna see it in my eyes
It's not gonna hurt me when you cry

I'm never gonna know what you go through
All the things I say or do
All the hurt and all the pain
One thing selfishly remains
I'm not gonna miss you

I felt like Glen wrote that song as a gift; it was his way of telling me not to worry about him. He knew I would take care of him. He knew I was the one who would be left with the pain and profound loss. I am thankful that Glen never knew what I went through.

The trial period at the memory community extended into many months. Though he remained there, in my heart I always wanted Glen back home. I know that sounds crazy, and I'm not saying at this point that I wasn't half-crazy. I tried my level best to stay sane. A friend reminded me of Ernest Hemingway's mantra, "grace under fire," and I strove to maintain my cool, but it wasn't easy. It was during this same period that our dear friend Steve Ozark, who had come to Glen's aid, contracted pancreatic cancer and within two short months was gone.

My own father had been ill for years. Every time I spoke with him on the phone, he made light of his condition. But when my stepmom Joni sent me a photo and I saw his emaciated condition, I was shocked. I immediately flew to their home in Austin. He was barely strong enough to take me in his arms. A few months later he was gone.

I was in Austin for Daddy's funeral when the memory community called to say Glen had turned violent with one of the caregivers and was in an ambulance headed to the psychiatric ward of a hospital. I rushed back to Nashville to meet with the psychiatrist who felt that Glen needed someone with him—a personal sitter—all during the day. If he became violent again, the memory community would expel him.

I asked my team if any of them knew of anyone who needed a job. Matt said he had a Pepperdine friend who wanted to move to Nashville. I hired Brody Wooton, a twenty-two-year-old PK (preacher's kid) from Texas, who had just spent two years helping run an orphanage in Guatemala. Brody moved in with us and became what I affectionately call one of my basement people or denizen of the lower level.

Brody was a good-looking surfer with shoulder-length blonde hair. On his very first day at work, Glen walked over to Brody, took his face in his hands, and gave him a great big kiss right on the mouth. Glen had mistaken Brody for me. Thankfully Brody had a great sense of humor. From that moment on, they were best buddies. Brody played guitar and sang for him every day. By then Glen could no longer play but would often launch into an "air guitar" solo to accompany him.

Brody was the only one able to get Glen into the shower. He took a few punches in the process, but he was strong, with fast reflexes, and didn't mind taking one for the team.

While the battle to keep Glen safe was ongoing, another battle was brewing, one I had not expected. It hit me like a ton of bricks.

CHAPTER 25

FRACTURED FAMILY

From the day I married Glen in 1982, I adopted a policy to reach out and embrace the five children he had fathered before we met. That policy never changed. I invited them, their spouses, and their children, whom I called my own grandchildren, to all the big family functions. They were always welcome in our home. I urged Glen to spend as much time with them as he could. We invited them to concerts; we took them on many tours; we cherished their presence. I may have even over-compensated in this area because I knew that Glen carried guilt for not spending enough time with them. I wanted to help him remove that guilt. With three of his children, the love we offered was warmly received and returned. With two it was not.

One in particular, whom I simply refer to as the adversary, took a video of Glen in the late stages of Alzheimer's in the sanctuary of his HIPAA-protected memory community and gave it to the press. She claimed I wasn't taking care of him or visiting him. I was there every day! Then one of her half siblings joined her in a suit asking for conservatorship, control of all our assets, and the right to move Glen to another state. Just like that, I had a major legal fight on my hands. Before, I had only one adversary. Now I had two.

I was being accused of "secluding from the family" my seventy-eight-year-old husband and, even more, prohibiting the family "from participating in his care and/or treatment." That report came from the Associated Press.

I had never, not once, kept any family member from Glen at any time. I had done the opposite. The more family, the better. Furthermore, Glen had given me, his wife of over thirty years, his care power of attorney, and power of attorney to our three children if something happened to me. The last thing in the world anyone needed was intra-family feuding, especially in light of the fact that the doctors said Glen could have less than a year to live.

I had no choice. I had to engage in legal combat. To do so cost a fortune. It had cost another fortune to give Glen the kind of care he required. But this wasn't the time to think of money. My only thought was of Glen. My adversaries had no earthly notion how to deal with a man in the final stage of Alzheimer's. Even as Glen was dying, I had to fight for his life.

I won the long and bloody legal battle. I was awarded conservatorship, and my adversaries were even sued by their own lawyer. The nightmare got darker. A hate page on Facebook created by an unknown party restated the same lie that I'd never allowed Glen's children from his previous marriages to visit him, this in spite of the fact that I had never once denied any family member a visit. To the credit of Facebook, they took down the hate page only to have a new one pop up under a new name, a page that was also removed. Yet the nightmare continued.

"Somehow" trolls found out Glen's location. Some showed up pretending to be family members. Others began calling in bogus complaints of elder abuse and neglect to adult protective services. This harassment created an unnecessary amount of work and strain on the community's administration and staff, but they stood by me and supported me throughout visits from the ombudsman and my own legal ordeal.

As if that wasn't enough fun for them, the trolls put up Wanted

Dead or Alive posters of me on Facebook, resulting in dozens of death threats. Every time I showed up to visit my husband, I worried that someone might shoot me. Glen's safety, my safety, and that of the other residents there had been compromised. I grew afraid. I put up twenty-four-hour surveillance cameras around my house.

Brody spent most of the ensuing year watching over Glen during his waking hours. I took over at dinner so that I could put Glen to bed and kiss him good night. The only problem was Glen never stayed in bed. One night, when a night care partner was trying to direct him back to his room, he punched her in the face. The nurse called me at 2:00 a.m. They loved Glen and did not want to traumatize him by sending him back to geriatric psych again. At the same time, they were legally designated as assisted living and not licensed to care for violent residents.

That's when I decided to fulfill my heart's desire and bring Glen back home.

The first night I lay down next to him and for a moment tried to pretend that things were like they used to be before Alzheimer's. I snuggled up into his arms. I felt battered and broken. To my dismay, he didn't respond. I cuddled him anyway. I needed him. I missed him. I drifted off to sleep only to wake up an hour later to find both of us soaking wet. I spent the next hour cleaning him with a washcloth, changing his clothes, dodging punches, changing the sheets, and cajoling him to lie back down. Heartbroken, tired, and depressed, I climbed into my own bed across the hall and turned on the "pell-mell bell." So much for my honeymoon fantasy.

Glen required constant supervision—every second of every minute of every day. Exhaustion started to settle in again. I was once more reminded why Dr. Peter Rabins titled his well-known guide for caregivers, *The 36-Hour Day*. Even with my trusted team helping me whenever they could, Glen was more out of control than ever.

During these gruesome days, I also grew afraid of Glen. One night he socked me in the face and gave me a black eye. I didn't take it personally because it wasn't personal. By then he didn't know who I was or what he was doing. He was simply striking out. This time, on the advice of Glen's personal doctor, my home care team and I took him to Vanderbilt Psychiatric Hospital.

I knew I couldn't bring Glen back home again, and I didn't want to endanger or burden the community again. Then I had an epiphany. When God closes a door, he opens a window. When I initially began researching memory care, I visited a construction site where a new community was about to be built in memory of Dr. Abram C. Shmerling, a prominent physician who had died in 2006 after an eleven-year battle with Alzheimer's. Frustrated with the quality of care available to his father during the late stages of the disease, Michael Shmerling spent nearly ten years researching current memory care philosophies, collaborating with designers, physicians, researchers, and gerontologists in an effort to develop a state-of-the-art care community in Nashville. Early in the process, Michael became so passionate about the project that he and another prominent Nashville philanthropist endowed the Vanderbilt University Abram C. Shmerling, MD Chair in Alzheimer's and Geriatric Medicine—the first endowed chair at a major medical university with Alzheimer's as its focus. Their concept was amazing, but in 2014 it would be a year before Abe's Garden, named after the good doctor, would be completed. I immediately put Glen on the waiting list. That was eleven months ago. Within a month this state-of-the-art community would be opened and Glen would be its first resident. God's timing was perfect.

On August 27, 2015, my children and I attended an appreciation ceremony at Abe's Garden along with 220 other Nashvillians committed to elevating Alzheimer's care. I spoke a few words about my personal journey. Ashley and Shannon sang songs, as did Mary Chapin Carpenter and Alison Krauss. During the event, Ashley, Shannon, and I toured the state-of-the-art community that was ideal in every way, far beyond anything we could imagine. That evening I spoke with other women whose husbands had Alzheimer's. One of the women I met was Vicki Bartholomew, whose husband, Sam, once a prominent lawyer, would become one of Abe's first residents along with Glen.

Glen moved to Abe's Garden a month after the preopening event. I felt I had no choice. The sad truth is that my adversaries made it impossible for me to care for Glen at home even if I could have. If he fell, I feared they'd claim I'd pushed him. If he died, I feared they'd accuse me of killing him. Thankfully, Abe's Garden would do more than keep Glen safe; it would keep me safe as well.

Having a professional caregiving team gave me the freedom to focus on being Glen's wife again. I did what was best for Glen, me, and our children. I climbed into bed that night with peace of mind. I wasn't breaking my marriage vows; I was keeping them. I was taking care of my husband "in sickness," as I had "in health."

I never say I "put" or "placed" my husband in a "home" or "facility." Those terms feed a negative stigma that keeps people from getting the help they need. I say, "Our family joined a memory care community." It *was* our community too. During that time, we lived each day with families on the same journey who understood what we were going through. We laughed together, cried together, prayed together, and supported each other. If this disease becomes too difficult to manage at home, being part of a quality memory care community should be your first choice, not your last resort.

Abe's proved to be everything we hoped for. Matt and Brody were hired as full-time caregivers and completed an unparalleled training program. They would be there every day to help with Glen, maintaining valuable continuity. I marveled at how God had orchestrated so many things to come together at just the right time. My concern that Glen would not be able to benefit from the activities or programs proved wrong. Just sitting with a group of people gave him a sense of belonging, connecting him to the immediate world around him.

Vicki and I saw each other every day while visiting our husbands. We hoped that Glen and Sam would become friends and enjoy each other's company. That hope was completely squelched when Sam saw Glen in an altercation with Matthew and Brody. Glen needed to pee, so the boys were just trying to lead him to the bathroom, but he did not want to go with them. Glen roared at them and gave Brody a big shove. Matt and Brody had become Sam's buddies, and Sam, a West Point man and brawny former football player, was not about to let anything happen to them. He puffed up his chest and rushed over to rescue them. The boys defused the situation beautifully, but from that time on Sam did not like Glen. One day Vicki tried to walk Sam over to visit with us, but Sam stopped in his tracks and warned Vicki sternly, "Stay away from that guy. He's already killed two people!" Vicki and I just had to chuckle about the absurdity of it all.

Another day Glen walked up to Vicki and Sam and started

singing them a song in gibberish. Vicki did not recognize the melody but said that when Glen was through, he took a bow, curled up one side of his lips in a perfect Elvis impersonation, and said, "Thank you very much."

As days passed, I began to sense a calm I hadn't seen in months. Something about Abe's Garden soothed his soul. Part of that was due to his fascinating neighbors. One woman who had been a concert pianist still played magnificently. Another fine musician had worked as a conductor and arranger for Disney. Because he had a hard time with language, he made the sounds and motions of playing a trombone, a trumpet, or a xylophone— all to tell you to have a nice day. Glen and I both enjoyed our new eclectic and eccentric group of friends.

A week or so after he was settled into his suite, I was getting ready to leave the house for my daily visit when the doorbell rang. On the porch was a woman from adult protective services. She was there, she said, because of an anonymous tip that Glen was being abused. I invited her in, asking if she had any interest in looking over my file on recent events. She did. She examined the many death threats I'd received, the vicious Facebook posts, and the three police investigations stating that Glen was indeed well cared for. Beyond that, I urged her to visit him at Abe's Garden. She agreed to see the community for herself, and her glowing report was unambiguous: Glen was receiving the best possible care.

Part of my self-care entailed participating in a support group with women losing their mates to dementia. I was struck by the "deer in the headlights" gaze fixed upon each woman's face.

As they slowly began to share their stories, some cried, some remained stoic, and some seemed stuck in denial. Some had quit their jobs to stay home to care for their husbands. All had been grieving the slow loss of their husbands for years. Many felt that their friends and family did not understand the severity of their challenge. As the meetings continued, our hearts opened. Like me, like everyone, they required compassion. They needed to be heard. And they needed to know that they were not alone. When emotional pain is shared, the pain is easier to bear. This revelation led me to start a blog, lifestyle guide, and social movement called CareLiving.org, to inspire, encourage, and enpower caregivers to care for themselves while caring for others.

CHAPTER 26

DEEPER PAIN

CHAPTER 26

DEEPER PAIN

Not three months after Glen was settled at Abe's Garden, another bomb exploded. A bill was introduced to the Tennessee state legislature by an opportunistic state senator crippling a conservator's ability to protect their ward. Then things became more bizarre.

On January 27, 2016, my adversaries along with Tanya Tucker—*Tanya Tucker!*—appeared with the senator before the state assembly. My adversaries claimed they were allowed to visit Glen only twice a month. The truth is that they were allowed to visit him as many times as they wanted. The only caveat was that they adhere to the mediation agreement protecting Glen's privacy and dignity that they had voluntarily signed. Then Tanya addressed the assembly, as if dating Glen for ten months, thirty-five years before, qualified her to speak on his behalf. She commiserated with my adversaries before breaking out into song. Right then and there, like "a faded rose from days gone by," she croaked out "Delta Dawn." The situation was sheer lunacy.

Yet lunacy required a legal response. The next day my lawyer requested an emergency motion to the Probate Division of the Seventh Circuit Court to unseal the mediation paperwork from January 2015 in order to set the facts and stories straight before the Tennessee General Assembly, in response to the outrageous assault on my conservatorship. Meanwhile, my adversaries' own children wrote letters to the legislators urging them to disregard their parents' testimony. Glen's sisters, nephews, and nieces also fired off e-mails on my behalf.

Thankfully the Tennessee Bar Association successfully watered down the bill to protect conservators and their wards. Unfortunately, the senator attached an amendment to the bill at the last minute, naming the bill after my husband, though the bill had nothing to do with Glen at all. I was never even consulted. The formal signing by the governor was attended by my adversaries and—you guessed it—Tanya Tucker standing behind him. Magazines ran the story without asking me for comment.

As expected, my adversary showed up at Abe's Garden the next day, with a fan in tow, demanding to be let in and threatening to sue the community. I was called to ask how to handle it. I said please allow my adversary in but send the fan away. I then instructed my attorney to write my adversary, advising her that the bill had no impact on the visitation stipulations the court had ordered her to comply with. We sued her for contempt of the mediation agreement on multiple counts.

The battle raged on. That summer the *New York Post* published a hit piece against me that included defamatory statements about Glen's condition. I responded through counsel. I also dropped my jaw when Ms. Tucker came out with a song written by none other than the senator—payoff, I assume, for slipping Glen's name on his bill. Now the starstruck senator had his name associated with two celebs.

Ultimately, after tortuous twists and turns, the Campbell name was officially removed from the bill, though apologies were never made to me or the Campbell family. I was forced to spend another fortune on this absurdity, but I remain grateful that, in the end, justice prevailed.

My deepest gratitude goes out to Speaker of the House Beth Harwell, Speaker of the Senate Randy McNally, and Governor Bill Haslam, for righting the grievous wrong that was done to me, my husband, and our children. It would have been nice, however, to have received a public retraction, rather than sweeping it under the rug.

In my opinion, the Tennessee legislature should authorize an ethics investigation into this sordid state senator for exploiting the very people he was purporting to protect—people in need of a conservator.

CHAPTER 27

A BETTER PLACE

In July 2017, Glen had taken a turn for the worse. He could barely walk. He was at a high risk of falling at any moment. He could no longer coordinate enough to lift food or drink to his mouth. Feeding him was difficult and sometimes dangerous. He could easily aspirate. Every meal was an ordeal.

Hospice was required. Within days he lost the reflex to swallow and began pocketing his food in his cheeks like a chipmunk. We were so sad that we found ourselves crying all the time.

By the first week of August, we knew it was only a matter of days. The family flew in to be with him. Everyone was invited, including my adversaries.

On August 7, Glen's breathing had become so labored that hospice was administering morphine to keep him comfortable. Our hearts were shattered. None of us was getting much sleep. The staff at Abe's did their best to accommodate our large family, sending in food and drink. Then, out of the blue, we heard the most beautiful music you could ever imagine coming from the performance area in Abe's Garden's Music and Movement household, where Glen lived. A violinist and cellist from the Nashville Symphony had come to play a concert. I opened the door, allowing the beautiful sounds to float into the room. Glen looked so peaceful lying there. I prayed the music would minister to him. Though Glen had forgotten everything, God had not forgotten Glen. God was walking with him through the valley of the shadow of death and doing it with music.

August 8.

We were gathered around our beloved Glen, watching and waiting. Every time he stopped breathing, we stopped breathing with him. Every time he began, we nearly collapsed.

At 10:00 a.m., he drew his last breath.

I threw my arms around him and sobbed.

I thanked God for taking him to a better place.

The memorial at the Country Music Hall of Fame was beautiful, the tributes heartfelt. He was remembered as a titan of American music and a humble man of love for the Lord and love for people from every walk of life.

Mourning was a challenge for me. I realized I had been mourning the incremental loss of my husband for so many years that the finality of his death was difficult to process. The logistical details of the memorial and the many tributes helped to distract me but also kept me from facing my feelings.

Then an epiphany.

It was August 24. Ashley and I were invited to an eclipse party. Apparently Nashville was the best place on the planet to watch the first total solar eclipse to sweep across the United States in the last ninety-nine years. It was the first time I'd been in a purely social setting since Glen passed. For the first time I was introduced as Glen's widow. How strange the sound of those words! As we gathered together to watch the moon cover the sun, I felt like I was in the Twilight Zone. I remembered reading in Genesis that God created the sun and the moon "for signs, and for seasons, and for days, and years" (Genesis 1:14 KJV). I thought about the timing of this total eclipse coming right after Glen's transition. I wondered if there might be a sign in it for me.

Now, at the very moment the moon blocked the sun, we all witnessed a rare and eerie phenomenon called "shadow snakes," wriggling images on the travertine surrounding the outdoor pool where we were standing. During the two minutes of darkness that followed, I thought about the first Passover and how God used snakes and darkness to show his power and convince Pharaoh to let his people go free. After the eclipse, the shadow snakes came back a second time, only to vanish as quickly as they had appeared. I took it as a sign.

Glen was finally free. I also reaffirmed my belief that God's mysterious wonders are without end. Life is without end. Having defeated death, Christ has allowed us to quell our fear of death. Having risen from the grave, Christ has assured us that life is eternal.

I looked back at this extraordinary journey with my man and wept with amazement and gratitude. I met him when I was a young woman, naive and guileless. I fell in love quickly. I fell in love completely. He swept me off my feet. Then reality hit. He had problems. I had problems. He had a disease. My lack of sophistication kept me from realizing that it actually *was* a disease. The power of his artistry—the purity of his singing voice, the virtuosity of his guitar playing—had me continually believing that he could do anything. With this disease still running rampant, he brought me into a world of glamour for which I was unprepared. But the God of grace saw us both through. God cured him of that disease.

I thought the way forward was surely a period of peace and bliss. When that period proved short-lived, our life turned upside down. I had so much to surrender—confusion, anger, remorse, resentment. I had so much to learn. Although in many ways this second disease mirrored the first, it was vital to differentiate the two. That wasn't easy. Nothing was easy. But it was necessary. If I were to grow in God, I had to do God's will. I had to accept the life God had given me. I had to master—or at least try to master—the lessons God had set out before me. I had to transform into a different person.

The challenges never stopped. How could I possibly handle another one? Well, I could and I did. I now know that challenges never stop. Our job is to face them with courage. That doesn't mean fear isn't recognized. Fear must be given a voice. To pretend it isn't there is to empower it even further. I've learned to confess my fears but, at the same time, galvanize my resolve to walk through those fears.

Glen's visceral fears became as evident as his artistic genius. I witnessed those fears and did all I could to assuage them. Music tempered his fears and gave him, and the whole world, a taste of heaven on earth. Glen's music, I believe, will never die.

I also believe that in the deepest part of his soul, even with his memory vanquished, Glen longed for God. God longed for Glen, as God longs for us all. I long for Glen, and for God, and in that longing comes a final reunion. And in that reunion there is ongoing life and ongoing love.

I conclude with gratitude for you, my patient reader, for accompanying me on this journey, and to God Almighty for allowing this journey to unfold.

With all the wonders of his spirit still alive, Glen remains gentle on my mind.

ACKNOWLEDGMENTS

I want to thank:

My Father in Heaven and my Lord and Savior Jesus Christ / Yeshua HaMashiach, for giving me my daily bread and the grace and mercy to get through each day.

My brothers and sisters in Christ who held our family up in prayer throughout our journey.

D. Thomas Lancaster, Director of Education at First Fruits of Zion and pastor of Beth Immanuel in Hudson, Wisconsin, along with his wife, Maria, who prayed for me and helped me begin the process of writing this book.

Pastor Richard Jackson and Rabbi Jack Zimmerman.

The fans who loved Glen through his triumphs and failures and who prayed for both of us while Glen was sick.

My children Cal, Shannon, and Ashley, who stood with me through thick and thin.

Glen's son Dillon Campbell who has always been a blessing.

My nephew Matthew Monier and our friend Amanda Carungi, who, along with helping me care for Glen and providing much needed comic relief around the house, also helped me begin the process of writing down my story.

My grandchildren Jesse Olson, Jeremy Olson, Brittany Campbell, and Trevor Campbell, who supported me and vouched for me during my legal ordeals with my adversaries.

My young granddaughter Annaleise Wintermute, who has always been a ray of sunshine for me.

Brody Wooton, who lovingly cared for Glen and became part of our family.

Glen's siblings: Gerald Campbell, Shorty Campbell, Jane Rather, Barbara Frazier, and Sandra Brink, who loved me and supported me throughout my marriage to Glen in sickness and in health, and who continue to be a source of strength to me. They are my brothers and sisters.

A special thanks to Glen's niece and nephew (Barbara's children) Angela Frazier and Shane Frazier, Glen's nephew (Lindell's son) Johnny and his wife, Donnie Campbell, and Uncle Boo's daughter Anita Thomas, who did everything they could to fight off the internet bullies and to stand up for me in the courts and the letter campaign to the Tennessee legislature.

To Glen's niece Jherri Baere and her husband, Erick Baere, for all the fun times we had in Malibu and for taking care of Glen when I went house hunting in Nashville.

To Steve and LaDonna Campbell for their faithful care of the Campbell Cemetery and their loving assistance in laying Glen to rest.

Special thanks to my friend Matt Chait. As the artistic director, website designer, social media manager, and editor of CareLiving.org, Matt has magically been able to take my straw and spin it into gold.

ACKNOWLEDGMENTS

SPECIAL FRIENDS:

Carl Jackson and Lynn Williford—who fixed me up on a blind date with Glen in 1981

Our dear friend Jackie Autry

Alice and Sheryl Cooper—for their friendship and encouragement throughout the years

Mel and Beth Shultz—the best neighbors and friends we could have ever been blessed with

Dante Rossi—The Golf Angel

Steve Ozark—Caterer to the Stars

CAREER:

Glen's manager and friend for over 50 years, Stan Schneider

Glen's longtime publicist, Sandy Brokaw

My business manager, Kami Stone

Glen's legacy manager, TK Kimbrell

Glen's producer Julian Raymond, who helped Glen end his career with the recognition he deserved

Capitol Records

Dave Kaplan and Scott Seine of Surfdog Records

Our publicist for the Goodbye Tour, Bobbie Gale

Glen's tour manager, Bill Maclay

Glens musical director, TJ Kuenster

GLEN'S BAND:

Cal Campbell—drums

Shannon Campbell—guitar

Ashley Campbell—banjo, keys

Ry Jarred—rhythm guitar

Keifo Neilson and Siggy Sjursen—bass

ACKNOWLEDGMENTS

Richard Landers—sound

Brad Conyers—sound

Clancy and Jill Fraser and their son Aaron "Whistle Britches"—
security / bus driver / buddy to Glen

PCH FILMS:

James Keach—producer/director

Jane Seymour—executive producer

Trevor Albert—producer

Alisa Benora—editor

Alex Exline—director of photography

Kayla Thorton—producer

Julia Pacetti—publicist for Glen Campbell on *I'll Be Me*

Marc Cohen—PR

PROFESSIONAL SUPPORT:

My lawyers, Bill Harbison, Carolyn Schott, Jay Cooper, Lisa
Bloom

My book doctor, David Ritz

My editor, Webster Younce

And finally, Abe's Garden, who helped us navigate some of our
hardest days.

PERMISSIONS

"Unforgettable," by Irving Gordon, ©1951 (Renewed), All Rights
Outside the U.S. Controlled by Bourne Co., All Rights Reserved
International Copyright Secured, ASCAP.

ACKNOWLEDGMENTS

Reserved Used by Permission, Reprinted by permission of Hal Leonard LLC.

"A Better Place," Words and Music by JULIAN RAYMOND and GLEN CAMPBELL, Copyright© 2011 WC MUSIC CORP., ELEVEN AM MUSIC and BMG RIGHTS MANAGEMENT (US) LLC, All Rights on behalf of Itself and ELEVEN AM MUSIC Administered by WC MUSIC CORP. All Rights Reserved, Used By Permission of ALFRED MUSIC.

"A Better Place," Words and Music by Julian Raymond and Glen Campbell, (c) 2011 ELEVEN AM MUSIC, SONGS OF WINDSWEPT PACIFIC and GLEN CAMPBELL MUSIC, All Rights for ELEVEN AM MUSIC Administered by WC MUSIC CORP. All Rights for SONGS OF WINDSWEPT PACIFIC and GLEN CAMPBELL MUSIC Administered by BMG RIGHTS MANAGEMENT (US) LLC, All Rights Reserved Used by Permission, Reprinted by permission of Hal Leonard LLC.

"Strong," Words and Music by JULIAN RAYMOND and GLEN CAMPBELL, Copyright© 2012 we MUSIC CORP., ELEVEN AM MUSIC and BMG RIGHTS MANAGEMENT (US) LLC, All Rights on behalf of Itself and ELEVEN AM MUSIC Administered by WC MUSIC CORP. All Rights Reserved, Used By Permission of ALFRED MUSIC.

"Strong," Words and Music by Julian Raymond and Glen Campbell, Copyright (c) 2011 Songs Of Windswept Pacific, Glen Campbell Music and Eleven AM Music, All Rights for Songs Of Windswept Pacific and Glen Campbell Music Administered by BMG Rights Management (US) LLC, All Rights for Eleven AM Music Administered by WC Music Corp. All Rights Reserved Used by Permission, Reprinted by permission of Hal Leonard LLC.

"Remembering," Words and Music by ASHLEY CAMPBELL and

ACKNOWLEDGMENTS

ABOUT THE AUTHOR

Kim Campbell was married to legendary country-pop star Glen Campbell for thirty-four years until his passing in August 2017, following a long and very public battle with Alzheimer's. The award-winning documentary, *Glen Campbell: I'll Be Me*, shared their family's journey with the world and opened up a national conversation about the disease. Kim's work as an advocate for people with dementia and for their families has taken her to Capitol Hill and the United Nations, and she is the creator of a website called CareLiving.org that encourages, informs, and inspires caregivers to take care of themselves while caring for others. She also established the Kim and Glen Campbell Foundation to advance the use of music as medicine to unlock forgotten memories, restore and rebuild neural pathways, alleviate depression, manage behaviors, and boost cognition. Kim is an honorary faculty member of the Erickson School of Aging Studies, University of Maryland, Baltimore County, holds a BFA from East Carolina University, and studied interior design at UCLA.

To book Kim for speaking engagements, go to apbspeakers.com.

—